3/8/96

FRIENDS, ENEMIES AND SOVEREIGNS

Friends, Enemies and Sovereigns

by

Sir John Wheeler-Bennett
G.C.V.O., C.M.G., O.B.E., F.B.A.

With a Foreword by
Harold Macmillan

SBN 333 18168 9

First published 1976 by
MACMILLAN LONDON LIMITED
4 Little Essex Street London WC2R 3LF
and Basingstoke
Associated companies in New York Dublin
Melbourne Johannesburg and Delhi

Printed in Great Britain by
WILLMER BROTHERS LIMITED
Birkenhead

WITH HUMBLE DUTY

AND

BY GRACIOUS PERMISSION

I DEDICATE

THIS BOOK

TO

HER MAJESTY QUEEN ELIZABETH THE QUEEN MOTHER

WITH DEEP DEVOTION

JOHN WHEELER-BENNETT

Contents

Foreword

John Wheeler-Bennett completed his great series of historical writings by the publication in 1972 of *The Semblance of Peace*. These, taken as a whole, represent the life's work of a historian of the first order. In particular, *Brest-Litovsk*, *Hindenburg*, *Munich* and *The Nemesis of Power* together form a unique account of the tragedy that beset Germany and helped to destroy the civilised world. They more than established his reputation as an erudite and sagacious writer whose talents equalled all, and surpassed most, of his professional colleagues.

In addition, in the course of his long life he gave valuable and devoted service to the causes which he held dear, above all to that of Anglo-American co-operation in peace as in war. He was thus able to carry out, if in a somewhat unusual manner, his two main ambitions – to write history and, at least to some extent, to take part in making it.

Happily, in the last years of his life he yielded to the urgent request of his friends that he should tell us something of his own unusual and even romantic life. This he has done in three volumes. Two of these, *Knaves, Fools and Heroes* and *Special Relationships*, were published before his death. This one, *Friends, Enemies and Sovereigns*, has, alas, to appear posthumously. Fortunately the author was able to complete his task in spite of the pain and physical difficulties surrounding the last few months of his gallant life.

Each of these volumes has its special interest. Perhaps in this one the most dramatic passages are those dealing with the Nuremberg trials. Yet there is, for me, something that should be added to the picture which he presents of himself in these reminiscences. This is partly due to a certain shy reserve and indeed humility in his character; partly to a characteristic discretion. For instance, in ordinary conversation and interplay of friendly talk, although all of us were conscious of his vast knowledge based upon indefatigable labours, his part in discussion was always conducted with the lightest possible hand. Often he was more than interesting; he was deliciously gay and sometimes daring. He was one of the best talkers that I can remember, with a memory as retentive as even Churchill's. He was a superb raconteur and his fund of stories was as 'extensive and peculiar' as Mr Samuel Weller's knowledge of London. Thus the regret that I have about these volumes of his reminiscences is that they are too discreet. I would have liked to see on record some of the extraordinary tales with which he could fascinate us. Yet no doubt he judged rightly. There is a gulf properly fixed between the frivolity of the spoken word and the decorum of the printed text.

Perhaps I may be allowed, as one of his oldest and intimate friends, to try to add something to the picture of this remarkable man. He has been called a romantic, and indeed in the best sense of the word this is a true description. His life was an unusual one. It was rare for a small boy in the First World War to be blown up in his dormitory by a bomb. Yet this happened to him in April 1916 as the result of an air-raid upon his preparatory school when he was thirteen years old. It resulted in many years of ill-health. When I first knew him he still suffered from a painful stammer which caused him, with his sensitive nature, acute discomfort for many years. Again, it is rare for a young man enjoying a considerable private fortune to devote himself from earliest days to determination to become a historian and expert in international affairs. He resisted all the paternal pressure, which was more powerful in those days than now, to adopt a more conventional career. Hence his decision, apart from organising a *Bulletin of International Affairs*, to spend most of

might be called professional status he retained the enthusiasm and the panache of an amateur. He was indefatigable in pursuing the sources of his information from both books and people. Readers of these volumes will be astonished at the extraordinary variety of the people that he knew and to whom he talked, ranging from revolutionaries to monarchs. If, in a sense, he 'interviewed' some of these with the pertinacity of a professional journalist, he was only able to do so because by his charm he instantly won their confidence.

Finally, his high standards. I have known few authors even among the most professional who could equal his accuracy and persistence. Under the apparent ease there was an iron will which enabled him with so many disadvantages to achieve so much.

Thus it is that he will long be remembered as a man who in this modern world of scepticism and disillusion retained all his loyalties and enthusiasms. Indeed, from the beginning to the end of his life he was attached to deep beliefs, both in Church and State. In this sense perhaps he was a true romantic.

HAROLD MACMILLAN

Introduction

In this third volume of my recollections I have carried on the story of my life, which I began in *Knaves, Fools and Heroes* and continued with *Special Relationships*. This book begins with my forty-third birthday (13 October 1945), which Ruth and I observed in New York, and ends with my seventieth, which we celebrated in London at Brooks's. In it I give some account of my activities in the post-war years, during which I attended the Nuremberg Trials of the major war criminals, became British Editor-in-Chief of the captured archives of the German government, saw something of Berlin under the unique circumstances of the airlift, wrote various books and had the honour to be appointed the official biographer of King George VI. All these events entailed experiences and adventures, both grave and gay, and gave me further opportunities to see behind the scenes in modern history.

I am deeply honoured by and grateful to Her Majesty Queen Elizabeth the Queen Mother for graciously accepting the dedication of this volume.

In writing this book I have refreshed my memory by reference to my engagement books, letters and papers which I wrote and received during the period and such relevant documents as are to be found in the Public Records Office. I am, however, as always, greatly indebted to those of my friends who have read and criticised my manuscript in whole or in part. Chief among these are His Excellency Baron Gevers, Netherlands Ambassador to the Court of St James, Mr Harold Macmillan, Sir John Hunt, Sir Martin Charteris, Sir Robin Mackworth-Young, Lord Franks, Sir Patrick Dean,

INTRODUCTION

Dr James M. Hester, formerly President of New York University, and his wife Jannie, Clifton Child, Sir William Deakin, Anthony Nicholls, Dr Otto John and, last but by no means least, Aubrey and Constance Morgan. Their suggested and welcome amendments have in every case been of the greatest help to me and to my work and I am deeply grateful; needless to say, they are in no way responsible for the opinions I have expressed.

My special thanks are due to Rex Allen, who has not only reviewed the text in type but has also corrected the proofs, and also to Alan Maclean and Richard Garnett, of the house of Macmillan, for their invaluable editorial assistance.

Mrs Sybil Cook has once again performed prodigies of transliteration and has developed an almost uncanny ability to read my handwriting. I am deeply appreciative of all her help.

I must also acknowledge most gratefully the generous, understanding and efficient assistance which I have received from the staffs of the London Library and the libraries of the Royal Institute of International Affairs and the Imperial War Museum.

Finally my enduring gratitude belongs to my wife Ruth, who throughout the writing of these volumes has been my dearest and most effectively trenchant critic.

J.W.W.-B.

Garsington Manor,
Oxford

CHAPTER ONE

The Road Back

I spent my forty-third birthday, 13 October 1945, in New York. I had just been released from government service, having spent my war in both America and Britain, first as Personal Assistant to the British Ambassador, Lord Lothian, then in the British Information Services and finally in the Political Intelligence Department of the Foreign Office, of which I had ended up as Assistant Director-General, my boss being Sir Robert Bruce Lockhart. My last assignment, as I have described in *Special Relationships*, had been to wind up the assets of this department in New York.

I had been married seven months before, but of these I had spent less than two with my American wife, Ruth, having been snatched from her during our honeymoon and detained in England by the exigencies of war until after V-J Day, when I had rejoined her in New York.

Now I was master of my own destiny again – and I was fairly clear in my mind what I wanted to do. In the last weeks of the war I had been offered jobs in government service and in British and American universities. I had refused both because I wanted very much to write two books, the first on the Munich Crisis – of which I had already written a draft during a spell of sick leave in Mexico – and the second on the abortive conspiracy to assassinate Hitler and over-throw the Nazi regime on 20 July 1944. Both required much thought and careful planning, as well as copious research.

The Munich Crisis had been much in my thoughts during such spare time as I had for contemplation during the war and I had begun gathering material. Certain Czechoslovak statesmen had been in exile in America and I had talked

with them. Bruce Lockhart had taken me frequently to see
President Beneš at Aston Abbotts, his English residence, and
Jan Masaryk had not only told me much himself but had
promised me access to the Czech Government archives once
Prague had been liberated. He fulfilled this promise with all
generosity, and I made several visits to Prague after the war
before Czechoslovakia was submerged by the Communist
wave and Jan himself was murdered.

I felt, however, that before actually embarking on the
book as a serious enterprise I owed it to Lord Halifax, of
whose official family I had been a member and to whom
I owed certain kindnesses, to tell him what I proposed to do.
When, therefore, I paid him my farewell visit at the Embassy
in Washington and he asked me what I was going to do
now, I said frankly that I meant to write a book on the
Munich Crisis in the light of what had gone both before
and after.

The Ambassador sat silent for a moment in deep thought.
Then, 'Will I have to stand in a white sheet in the judgement
of history?' he asked. I replied that I thought a good many
people would have to do this and that he would probably
be among them. He paused again, and then said with that
delightful twisted smile, 'Well, my wivvers are quite un-
wung.' So might any great figure of the *ancien régime* have
entered the tumbril en route for the Place de la Guillotine
Lord Halifax was never lacking in panache.

With my hands thus freed and my conscience clear I felt
ready to begin work, but here a difficulty arose. In view of
my health, which had suffered considerably during the war,
my doctors in New York advised strongly against my return
to England for three or four months. Nor indeed was it
possible, in the then prevailing state of surface transport,
to get accommodation for ourselves and our immense collection of household goods which we were transferring to
England, and which themselves precluded air travel.

It was at this time of our dilemma that Isabella Greenway

King, of whom I have written in *Special Relationships*, came once again to our aid. She happened to own a house on the Connecticut coast, between Bridgeport and Fairfield, which, with her characteristic generosity, she placed at our disposal. It stood on a cliff overlooking the tiny harbour of Black Rock, protected and almost hidden from the water, yet with magnificent seascape views from many of its windows.

Its story, as retold to us by local inhabitants, was charming. In the splendid days of gilded tycoonery, the great financial and legal grandees used to commute in their steam yachts from their strange neo-Gothic houses on the Hudson River, set about with every conceivable architectural exaggeration, to the tip of Manhattan Island and thence by hansom cab to their offices in Wall Street. In the summer their week-ends would, as like as not, be spent at Newport, on the Rhode Island coast, where grandiose and sprawling mansions were designated 'cottages'.

One Saturday, three friends, each in his own yacht, sailed from New York's Battery destined for Newport. A sudden storm caused them to run for shelter and, by good fortune, they found sanctuary in the virtually unknown bay below the village of Black Rock. When the storm had blown itself out they landed and were delighted with what they found. A pleasant stretch of rolling grassland separated the cliff-top from the village, and the harbour beneath was safe and tranquil. Enchanted with their discovery, they agreed to buy up any available real estate and each would build his own house there according to his personal taste. (History does not record to what degree their wives were consulted in this venture.) There resulted a Touraine château, a Queen Anne mansion and something designed, I think, to represent a Tudor manor-house. It was a strange architectural hotchpotch to find on a Connecticut promontory.

In due course, Isabella Greenway King acquired the Touraine château. She was something of a collector of houses, her mother having once told her (as she herself subsequently told Ruth) that no lady ever stayed in a hotel, and now, in the winter of 1945–6, it was this singular but comfortable residence that she lent to Ruth and me, and where I began the second draft of *Munich, Prologue to Tragedy*.

We had a few neighbours and our only friends were Charles and Anne Lindbergh who lived nearby. It was now that Charles displayed a gratifying confidence in my discretion by placing at my disposal all his diaries of the pre-war period, including his accounts of his visits to Germany and France during the fateful summer of 1938, and especially the circumstances of the presentation to him of the German Order of Merit by Goering at a public banquet, which came as an unpalatable surprise to him. I also read of his talks with Bill Bullitt, then American Ambassador in Paris, and with the tragically divided members of the French cabinet, not to speak of his abortive conversations with officials in London. No historian could have dreamed of admission to such an Aladdin's cave of historical riches, which not only documented many of the controversial discussions which Charles and Aubrey Morgan and I had had during the war, but opened up fresh vistas of which I had been vaguely aware but never certain.

It may be thought, perhaps, that a New England winter was scarcely the most salubrious for a health cure, but it suited both Ruth and me very well. We were both very tired, our home was warm and comfortable, food was plentiful, and we could rest as much as we liked. Though we were snowed up for days at a time by blizzards – once having to be rescued by Charles Lindbergh from a drift into which I had inadvertently driven the car – we were then of an age to enjoy walking in the snow, though I must confess that I have outgrown that particular delectation.

It was an exceedingly pleasant episode in our lives and one which had enriched our love and gratitude to Isabella Greenway King and her family. But by the beginning of

1946 the log-jam of returning British from America had eased. I was able, through the kindly good services of Bill Donovan, to acquire comfortable accommodation for Ruth and myself, and freight space for our household belongings, on the *Queen Elizabeth* which sailed on 6 February. As we boarded I was handed a cable from my sister announcing the death of our mother, who had been a hopeless invalid for some years.

Though I had been a householder and taxpayer in England since attaining my majority, I had led so peripatetic a life that, with the exception of one year during the war, I had not spent six consecutive months in London for over twenty years. Moreover I had never exercised my franchise. Having been domiciled for most of my adult life in the constituency of St George's, Westminster, I had been represented by Duff Cooper, who, having fought a fierce battle in 1931, was well able to hold his seat without help from me. Indeed I never recorded my vote in a general election until 1951, because in 1945, though in England, I was still registered as a non-resident.

I was therefore almost as rootless as an alien, save for the deep affection which had always existed between my sister and myself, and I had to learn again, in many respects, the customs of my country, to which, although I was intensely loyal and devoted, I felt a stranger.

For Ruth, of course, it was worse still. She had visited England on a number of occasions but had never made a home there. Moreover she too had been on overseas service in the Middle East for the last three years and the problems of keeping house in a strange land, where nearly every domestic convention was totally different from that of her native country, had been prodigious. I have never admired anything more than the way in which she navigated those uncharted seas, under circumstances in which, because of my own long absence, I could be of little help to her.

Together we faced the new world of Britain in the middle forties: a Britain tired and war-weary, yet compelled to face the severities of continued wartime shortages while deprived of the continued wartime stimulus. I shall never forget the dour drabness of those years, the greyness of one's daily existence, the seemingly endless nightmare of a Labour Government struggling manfully to solve the inevitable problem of post-war reconstruction, yet electing to embark simultaneously and precipitately upon the completion of the Social Revolution which had begun with Lloyd George's 'People's Budget' of 1909.

Food was scarce, scarcer than it had been in wartime. Bread was rationed for the first time in our national history, and had it not been for the food parcels which Ruth's mother so generously sent us from America we should have been hard pressed indeed. As it was we were able to share our blessings with our less fortunate friends and neighbours. One still queued for nearly everything, and coupons were required for most commodities, including clothes and petrol.

In the spring of 1946 we established ourselves in Garsington Manor, some few miles from Oxford, which my sister and her husband, Trevor Heaton, then a don at Christ Church, had acquired from Philip and Lady Ottoline Morrell in 1926. Under the Morrell dispensation the place had acquired a certain literary notoriety which, in later years, has developed into something of a cult. It is no purpose of mine to discuss here the merits or demerits, the vices or the virtues, of the Bloomsbury Group. I never knew them, and have little sympathy with the lack of gratitude which many seemed to have evinced toward their generous patroness, whose warm hospitality they had not hesitated to accept as open-handedly as it was offered. It must be confessed, however, that the recent fascination which this curious group of intellectual phenomena exercises upon students of a lost age has impinged upon the peace and privacy of the present incumbents.

It may well be that, in the days of Irene and Trevor Heaton, Garsington lacked the literary distinction of the previous era but it also lacked its intellectual felinity. During those later pre-war years, when I knew it well, Garsington became the centre of hospitality for professors, dons and students from the University of Oxford. It was essentially a happy house and its owners were well loved. In its way it represented a style of gracious living which vanished with the march of Hitler's field-grey legions into Poland in September 1939.

During the war the place was let, and it became our property in 1945 because my sister and her husband wished to continue living in Oxford. I bought it from them by cable from America over Ruth's protest that she did not like Elizabethan houses. She withdrew her objections, however, when I explained that, because of the lack of housing in post-war England, we were lucky to get any house. We have welcomed there many friends from all parts of the world and of a most catholic variety – politicians and statesmen, churchmen, diplomats and historians, together with academic figures, both dons and students, from many countries, and particularly from our beloved University of Virginia.

Garsington has been described so frequently and in such detail in recent works that further comment from me is unnecessary. It has been called one of the finest examples in England of the small Elizabethan manor-house and garden. Be that as it may, the whole credit for the maintenance of standards must go to Ruth, who has laboured nobly in this interest. In addition to being a warm and successful hostess, she has in her blood an inherent love of the soil and of its products, whether they be roses or artichokes, and is wonderfully successful in tending them. I am by nature neither a countryman nor a gardener, and though, without undue presumption, I share with the Almighty a pleasure in walking in a garden in the cool of the evening, since for medical reasons I no longer ride a horse, I am happiest when I have the pavements of London or New York beneath my feet. I have reached that stage of life when I like to be within walking distance of a good pharmacy and a good bookshop.

It was early summer before we were settled and in a position to have people to stay, and among our first week-end visitors was 'Moley' (Sir Orme) Sargent, then Permanent Head of the Foreign Office. In writing of Moley I see him as a survival of a past age, almost an anachronism. In appearance, tradition, conventions, standards and values he was essentially Edwardian, with all the elegance and *élan* of that period. Tall, thin and aristocratic, he had a caustic and cynical wit which could be blasting and a quizzical sense of humour which could be hilarious. He had great distinction and a rigid idea of what was socially acceptable – and what was not. During one of his frequent visits to Garsington a don had bicycled out from Oxford, having invited himself for tea, and was shown into the drawing-room bare-legged and in the briefest of cycling shorts; Moley rose and left the room with ostentatious disgust and did not return until our caller had departed.

Moley's mind was one of the most diverting. He was widely read and his memory was stored with delightful reminiscences and anecdotes. One never talked with him without adding to one's knowledge in some unexpected way and he could be the best and funniest of companions. He was a delightful guest and an excellent host.

Of course, he also had his defects. A sickly only child, he had survived, somewhat surprisingly, some years at Radley, but had never been to university. Instead he had been educated abroad, becoming highly proficient in French and German. Delicate health and a certain natural superiority had given him a deceptive appearance of conceit. It is true that he had a sardonic smile worthy of Swift himself and that he did not suffer fools gladly – or indeed at all – but neither did he, like some, see a fool blooming by every stone. However, his contemporaries in the Foreign Office were apt to describe him as 'stand-offish' and his subordinates were frankly frightened of him. He also had a bachelor's tendency to selfishness in respect of comforts and in later years became something of an old maid, but he remained for years one of our dearest friends and his death in 1962 caused a gap in our lives which has never been filled.

In his profession Moley had been brilliant and far-seeing, though perhaps with too great an inclination to pessimism. I had known him since those fateful days of the Munich Crisis in the summer of 1938, and I knew how deeply his sense of integrity had been outraged by those events. His feeling of guilt towards the Czechs was later repeated towards the Poles, whom he felt Britain had deserted and betrayed. He sought to make personal amends after his retirement by staffing his charming William and Adelaide house in Bath with countless Poles, who seemed to justify Bismarck's comment on their countrymen that 'they bred like rabbits'. During the years of the war when he and Bruce Lockhart had been joint Deputy Under-Secretaries at the Foreign Office I had seen much of him, and now he had succeeded Sir Alexander Cadogan as Head of the Office.

His first visit to us at Garsington had an important effect on the next stage of my career. I was still working on *Munich* and had recently been over to Paris to stay at the British Embassy, where Duff Cooper had allowed me to read his diaries of the period, which gave a vivid account of cabinet proceedings at that time – they may not find their equal even in Dick Crossman's journals. These had helped me immensely, but I was still fretting to get my hands on the German documents which were frequently being quoted in the press as emanating from the trials of the Nazi leaders then in process at Nuremberg, and of which many had a direct and vital bearing on my subject.

I remember complaining to Moley that copies of these documents were not available in London and that one had to depend on the abridged versions printed in the newspapers. His reply was characteristic:

'But why aren't you *at* Nuremberg?' he asked. 'Weren't you originally on the War Crimes Executive? Well then, you've got a perfect right to be there and I think they'll be glad to have you. I will telephone to our man on the prosecution team on Monday and the Foreign Office shall arrange your passage.'

Thus it was that within a couple of days I found myself airborne from Croydon airport en route to Nuremberg.

CHAPTER TWO

Nuremberg, 1945-6

Much has already been written by lawyers, historians and politicians on the Nuremberg Trials of the major war criminals; much more will doubtless be written in the future. It is improbable that agreement will ever be reached, but at least the subject has provided a happy hunting ground for many. I have made my own small contribution as a historian in *The Semblance of Peace* and I shall therefore repeat little of it here except as personal reminiscence. But I feel disposed to reiterate certain fundamentals in which I believe implicitly.

In the first place, I believe that, within the connotation of *1066 and All That*, the Nuremberg Trials were 'a good thing' rather than 'a bad thing'. Some sort of reparation had clearly to be made; some sort of punishment had to be meted out. The choice lay between summary court martial and a firing squad or the full dignity of legal procedure, and if it be a question of setting a precedent, I prefer the latter. Lawyers do, and will continue to, dispute the legal viability of the trials, but few have seriously suggested that it would have been better to shoot the defendants in a ditch.

Moreover few, if any, have questioned the essential fairness of the proceedings, certainly not the defendants or the counsel. They could query the competence of the International Military Tribunal to try them, but once this was established they did not hesitate to pay tribute to the justness of the trial. Indeed it was deeply impressive, and it was an important factor that every charge in the indictment (with one significant exception, of which I shall write later) was substantially documented from the official archives of the

German Government itself. The Nazi leaders and the agencies which they had created were tried and sentenced – or in some cases acquitted – on evidence provided by themselves.

It would, of course, have been cosier and more convenient for everyone if we had not had the Russians there, but how could we have avoided it? After all, they had been a powerful force in defeating the Wehrmacht and their position as a major ally could not be gainsaid. It was neither practical nor possible to exclude them, and, as it turned out, they proved themselves able and effective colleagues on both the level of the tribunal and of the prosecution – until the last moment brought their judges into disrepute.

The blot which the Russians had inflicted upon the record of the Nuremberg indictment, to which I have already referred, was the Katyn massacre. A few details are necessary. In September 1939, consequent upon their infamous pact of 23 August, Germany and Russia entered into a secret agreement for the fourth partition of Poland and this duly became a fact after the Soviet invasion of 17 September. Almost at once the Soviet authorities deported about one-and-a-half million Poles to Siberia but segregated some 15,000 officers within their former country, many of whom were later dispersed to various prisoner-of-war camps and shot. In June 1941 the Nazi Government treacherously attacked the Soviet Union and occupied their part of Poland, including the forest of Katyn. Some two years later, in April 1943, acting upon rumours, the local authorities exhumed the uniformed bodies of some 4500 Polish officers, many of whom had been shackled before death and had been shot in the back of the head.

Nothing could have been more advantageous to Nazi propaganda. The story was given maximum coverage and the world was stunned. The Polish Government-in-exile in London broke off diplomatic relations with Moscow and placed their embassy in the charge of the Australian chargé d'affaires, who happened to be my friend Keith Officer. The

Soviet Government denounced the whole thing as a Nazi plot. The German Government demanded an impartial enquiry by the International Committee of the Red Cross, and when this was refused by the Soviet Union appointed an International Medical Committee under the chairmanship of the Swiss pathologist, Professor Naville. A unanimous report was handed in that the mass-murder could not have been committed later than the spring of 1940 – at a time when only the Russians had been in possession of the Katyn area and some fifteen months before the German occupation.

When in 1944 the Red Army again held Katyn the Soviet Government appointed an all-Russian committee of enquiry which announced with unhesitating conviction that the massacre had been committed by the German army in the autumn of 1941, a verdict that did not gain a wide degree of acceptance.

It has always seemed to me that the Russian jurists who were actually at Nuremberg were not happy about the inclusion of the Katyn massacre in the indictment, but they were acting under direct and adamant orders from Moscow and, as such, had no choice. They did not introduce their demand for inclusion until the last few moments of the last meeting of the prosecuting staffs who were preparing the indictment, and it was only added after the British and Americans, Sir David Maxwell Fyfe and the Hon. Robert Jackson, had expressed their strong opposition. This was based on the sound legal argument that, whereas all the items of the indictment were founded on the evidence of authentic German documents supported by the evidence of reliable witnesses, the charges relative to the Katyn massacre rested on neither of these, but upon the mere assertion of the Soviet Government, lacking, as Jackson pointed out, anything which 'would meet the high standards of credibility required in a criminal trial'. While acceding to the Soviet demand, the British, American and French prosecutors made it clear that they would have no part in the conduct of this part of the indictment.

On the Tribunal the reaction to the Katyn affair was the subject of serious dissent, and despite the support given by General Nikichenko for the arguments of the Soviet prosecutor, no findings were made in the judgement as to the responsibility for the murders.

By and large, however, the co-operation of the Russians was good, and it is a fact that when what had been hailed as 'Quadripartite Solidarity' was crumbling into ruins in the world at large, it remained in existence in the legal vacuum of Nuremberg longer than anywhere else. For example, I believe it to have been impossible anywhere else to hear, as I did one day when lunching with the Tribunal, a British judge, Sir Norman Birkett, through an interpreter, chaffing a Russian judge, Colonel Volchkov, on the subject of Churchill's Fulton Speech of 5 March 1946.

On that June morning as I flew to Nuremberg I was possessed by some degree of uncertainty as to how to proceed when I got there. I had no status. Ostensibly I was in search of documents for my book, but that was a matter of private research and I was entering here a military area where passes were *de rigueur* and regulation sacrosanct. My only claim to official recognition was that I was on the plane at all, since air transit to Nuremberg was strictly confined to those engaged on public business. Moley Sargent had murmured that 'our man' in Nuremberg was a pleasant young man called Patrick Dean, from the Legal Department of the Foreign Office, to whom he had dropped a line, but I knew from my war-service how wary professionals are of amateurs in such circumstances as these and how ingeniously obstructive they could be on occasion.

However, I am a great believer in the Socratic dæmon and in allowing him to take command of a situation. In addition I have also a mystical counsellor whom I call to myself 'Balaam's Ass' and to whose advice I have long learned to listen and obey.

Both would appear to have been working overtime on that particular day. I was met by an R.A.F. car and driver, who welcomed me with some deference and whisked me away to an unknown destination. Relieved to find that I was at least expected, I was ready to pursue whatever course my dæmon led me.

It has been widely believed that the choice of Nuremberg as the seat of the International Military Tribunal was because of its close association with the zenith of National Socialist triumphs. Hitler had indeed made full play with the pride of place which the city had occupied in German history, both as a favourite place of residence of the Holy Roman Emperors and as guardian of the Imperial Regalia. While Munich had remained the headquarters of the Nazi movement, Nuremberg became the national show-ground of the Party. It was from here that Julius Streicher had published in *Der Stürmer* his odious and obscene libels against the Jews. Here was the centre of those vast pageants at which the Führer spoke *ex cathedra, urbi et orbi*, to his followers. Where the sweet voices of Hans Sachs and other Meistersingers had once re-echoed, there had resounded the fierce chorus of 'Horst Wessel Lied', cacophonously roared with fanatical fervour by the S.A. and S.S. Here had marched the sun-tanned paladins of the Labour Service battalions and the glowing faces of the Hitler Jugend. Here in the gigantic arena which Albert Speer had erected to the greater glory of National Socialism, Hitler had given to Germany the infamous laws of anti-semitism; here again he dangled before his cohorts the bright prizes of ultimate *Lebensraum* in the Ukraine and beyond the Urals; here too he had threatened Czechoslovakia with extinction and the world with war.

This congeries of circumstances would have been enough in itself to justify the establishment of the seat of the International Military Tribunal at Nuremberg, and indeed it had not been absent from the minds of those whose duty it was to make the choice, but the ultimate selection had been influenced more by pragmatic factors. Almost alone within the Reich, Nuremberg possessed those facilities necessary for the task involved. Not that it had escaped bombing. When American troops entered it in April 1945, it was pronounced by experts as 'ninety-one per cent dead'. Nevertheless, the capabilities existed. These included a large jail in a fair state of repair and a witness-house capable of holding the many who would be called upon to testify. In addition, housing accommodation was needed for the judges of the Tribunal, the prosecuting and defence counsel, the court staff, the hosts of pressmen and the considerable number of distinguished visitors who descended upon the city – not to mention the quartering of the large contingent of American troops and military police attached for guard duty. Above all, Nuremberg possessed a court-house of requisite size not only for the public sessions of the trial but for the offices of the members of the Tribunal and the prosecution teams and all the paraphernalia of a court of justice in full action. Within four months the United States Corps of Engineers had effected a series of miracles of improvisation and reconstruction which made it possible for the Tribunal to begin its duties on 20 November.

It was to the Palace of Justice that I was now driven and, on giving my name, was conducted down a series of corridors, with which I was to become thoroughly familiar during the weeks that followed, to a room where I found a blond young man in his late thirties bearing the unmistakable stamp of the Foreign Office. This was Patrick Dean, and the warmth and kindness with which he welcomed me indicated that Moley Sargent had given me a 'good character'. Pat himself had been working on the question of war crimes from its earliest days and had been a member of the British delegation to the Yalta Conference and also to the London Conference of Jurists in the summer of 1945. He now said that he had already spoken about me to the leader of the British prosecuting team, Sir David Maxwell Fyfe, who wished to see me on the following morning, and in the meantime a pass had been prepared for me giving the privilege of membership of the team, which included the right to sit at the prosecution table. I was thus given official status. As there was no room for me in the villa in which the British team was housed, I had been booked into the Grand Hotel, the semi-official hostelry maintained by the Americans, but I was invited to dine in the British mess.

Pat and I took to one another like ducks to water and a friendship was forthwith established between us which has lasted and, if possible, increased with the passage of time, and has been happily extended to include our wives. During the next years Ruth and I were to receive many kindnesses and much generous hospitality from Pat and Patricia Dean.

That evening I was to meet men who, though I had never met them before and was no lawyer myself, gave me the warmest of welcomes – with one exception – and went out of their way to make me feel at home and one of them. They cross-questioned me on my experiences in Germany during the pre-war years and my personal knowledge of the accused, and what I told them seemed to be accepted as being helpful. Every man there that evening (with, oddly enough, the single exception of the one individual who remained hostile to me!) was destined for high promotion and honours in the years to come. Pat Dean became the British member on the Security Council of the United Nations, and, after the somewhat precipitate termination of his service in that post in deference to Socialist policy, became Ambassador in Washington till his retirement in 1969. Harry Phillimore, deputy leader of the team, became a Lord Justice of Appeal. Elwyn Jones now graces the Woolsack as Lord Chancellor of England and Mervyn Griffith-Jones is Common Serjeant in the City of London. Truly it was a forcing ground of genius and distinction.

In passing, I must mention one other young Englishman who made, as it were, his debut at Nuremberg – Airey Neave, then a thirty-year-old barrister with a cherubic countenance which made him look even younger than he was. Perhaps to counterbalance this he affected a somewhat fierce and austere manner, but I always enjoyed his company. He had been called to the bar shortly before the war and had made his name as a sort of military Houdini by effecting a sensational escape from Colditz, the famous German prisoner-of-war camp. He was now Marshal of the Court to the Tribunal and in this capacity had served the indictment on Goering and his co-defendants. We became good friends and he subsequently was returned to the House of Commons for Abingdon, a neighbouring constituency to ours. At Nuremberg, however, where I saw a good deal of him, neither he nor I could foresee that thirty years later he would become Margaret Thatcher's campaign manager in her contest to oust and then to replace Ted Heath as leader of the Conservative Party, and become a member of her Shadow Cabinet.

The Grand Hotel, when I eventually reached it late that evening, proved to be in itself out of the ordinary. Not that one expected the ordinary in Nuremberg in the year of grace 1946, but there was something about the place which seemed to me to be macabre and almost sinister. In its palmy days it had been one of the leading hotels of the city and one in which foreign V.I.P.s invited to the Nazi Party rallies were housed. It had been badly damaged, however, and its resuscitation was another of the miracles performed by the American army. It was clean and though sparsely furnished was tolerably comfortable. The food was plentiful and, by American army standards, well cooked. It also sported a not undistinguished cellar which seemed to have survived the horrors of war remarkably well, and one was grateful for this because every mouthful of water was so heavily chlorinated that a spoon placed in a glass of it would stand alone, as they used to say of kitchen tea in the days of my youth.

This hygienic precaution was very necessary. The United States Corps of Engineers, though they had done marvels, had had only four months in which to perform them. They had had to confine their reconstruction operations to the barest minimum commensurate with the needs of the Tribunal, and these had not included clearing the ruins throughout the whole city. Many acres of rubble remained as they had fallen, and beneath them lay hundreds of bodies, a fact which became strongly and painfully apparent as the heat of the summer increased. Any measures, therefore, which could safeguard the outbreak of a serious epidemic were more than justified.

It was the ground floor, however, and therefore one's first impression, which was so oddly incongruous. This was the part of the hotel which had suffered least from the bombing and its restoration at the hands of the military had resulted in the appearance of nothing so much as a Hollywood set for an international spy drama. There was a good deal of red plush and artificial marble and tarnished ormolu, and there was nowhere to sit except in the reception hall.

What added to the Hollywood atmosphere was the clientele. Here were found officers in the uniforms of nearly every allied nation – I even saw a Brazilian colonel there on one occasion – for, besides the four major powers who appointed the judges, many of the smaller states whose territories had been occupied by the Nazis had attached minions to the Tribunal to watch over their special interests. In addition there were journalists from all over the world, officials of the court itself, and transient V.I.P.s from many countries. Before and after dinner the hall of the Grand Hotel was filled with a polyglot assortment of persons who gathered into groups that seemed to assume an amoebic activity, dividing and reuniting in a haze of alcohol and tobacco smoke.

B

It was part of the folklore of the Grand Hotel that in the period which followed the opening of the trials in November 1945, a Soviet officer had staggered through the revolving doors one evening and collapsed in a pool of blood on the floor of the hall, where he almost immediately died. It was found that he had been shot through the chest, but whether by an intoxicated Soviet comrade or a vengeful German was never known. The incident, I was told, caused the merest ripple among those already in full voice.

Another rather gruesome factor of the Grand Hotel was its cabaret. The management had decided that their guests required such entertainment, and had consequently called out of retirement a number of artists, dancers, comedians, singers, jugglers, etc., with which to regale them. To one like myself, who had known the wit and spice of the political cabaret life in Berlin during the Weimar period, this provincial unrehearsed mimicry was sheer mockery. In addition there was something infinitely tragic in these underfed entertainers in their pathetic and tarnished finery, singing their songs of the pre-Nazi period with desperate nostalgia and going through their several acts with wooden unspontaneity born of long years of absence from the stage during the Third Reich, when cabaret was considered among the decadences of Weimar.

I only attended a couple of these performances for I found them too depressing. In fact I found the whole atmosphere of the Grand Hotel deeply inimical to me personally and incongruous with the general purpose of our being at Nuremberg. Within a mile of the hotel a score of the former leaders of the Third Reich were being tried for their lives, charged with fearful crimes based on evidence which had shocked the civilised world. Outside the hotel, often flattening their noses against the cracked glass panels, were starving, or at any rate underfed, Germans. Inside, we, their conquerors who had brought their leaders to trial, were disporting ourselves in a manner certainly vulgar and virtually callous. I am no puritan and I trust I am not a prig, but there seemed to be something oddly offensive about it all. I am glad to say that I was not alone in this.

Later on I was 'liberated' from the ghoulish atmosphere of the Grand Hotel through the kindness of an old friend, Francis Biddle. I had known him in Washington when he had served as Attorney-General in President Roosevelt's administration. Slight of build, sharp of tongue and bright of intellect, Francis had been one of the many brilliant lawyers, including Dean Acheson, who had begun their careers as clerk to that almost legendary figure, Justice Oliver Wendell Holmes of the Supreme Court, who as a young officer during the American Civil War had saved President Lincoln's life by pulling him out of the line of fire, with the somewhat disrespectful injunction, 'Get down, you fool!' Francis was now the senior American judge on the International Military Tribunal. As such he had been allotted a large villa on the outskirts of Nuremberg where he lived alone, for his wife, Catherine, a charming woman and a poetess of distinction, had elected to stay at home. I accepted his invitation with alacrity and remained there until the end of the trial. A little later we were joined by another old friend of mine, Rebecca West, who was representing a British national newspaper, and the three of us made a very agreeable company.

After the dispersal of the Tribunal Francis Biddle stayed with Ruth and me at Garsington, and both he and Catherine were among the people whom we always looked forward to seeing during our visits to Washington when Pat and Patricia Dean were at the Embassy there.

Early on the morning following my arrival I met David Maxwell Fyfe for the first time. He was an impressive but amicable figure, sitting behind a wide writing desk. What struck one first about him was the size of his head, which was large and egg-shaped with a deep indentation in the forehead, the result of a motor-accident. His complexion was sallow but he had a charming smile and his eyes were kindly, except when on occasion they took on the hardness of agate. It was the same with his voice. Normally it had a pleasing sweetness of cadence, but when cross-examining it assumed a silky, steely quality which sent a twinge of fear through me even when acting as his assistant, and which I have seen reduce a victim on the witness stand to a state of pulverised terror. I have always regretted that I was not present to see his defeat of Goering on that celebrated occasion when the Reichsmarschall had 'made a monkey' out of the chief American prosecutor, Robert Jackson, and David had deflated him. In a few quiet sentences he had wiped the arrogant smile off Goering's face and had substituted for it a white mask of baffled fury.

In these early days of the trial Goering was very full of himself and his arrogance displayed itself in a variety of unpleasant ways. General Erwin Lahousen, who after the *Anschluss* had been transferred from the Austrian Counter-Intelligence to the Abwehr, was the first witness called by the prosecution. His evidence was very damaging and at the end of it, as he left the stand, Goering remarked loudly to Ribbentrop, across the zombie-like figure of Hess, 'That's one we missed after 20 July.' Another witness, former S.S. General Bach-Zelewski, added his contribution to the toll of adverse testimony and as he passed the dock Goering leapt to his feet and spat full in his face.

Such was the spirit of braggadocio in which the Reichsmarschall faced Mr Justice Jackson when the latter opened his cross-examination. Jackson had been on the Supreme Court bench for some four years and before that had been U.S. Attorney-General – an office which calls for little practice in advocacy – for a considerable time. Therefore his sixth sense of the cross-examiner, that subconscious instinct which immediately responds to the workings of a witness's brain, was inevitably somewhat sluggish and out of date. He also lacked the background of European history and the workings of European governments which was necessary for the effective use of the documents, and therefore laid himself open to Goering's crafty ripostes. Moreover he, too, was over-confident. Having previously dismissed with ease the evidence of two German Field-Marshals, von Brauchitsch and Milch, he gravely under-estimated the infinitely superior mentality of Goering.

Within ten minutes of the opening of the court duel it was apparent to all that Jackson was on the defensive. For almost two days Goering held the centre of the stage and dominated his opponent, eventually going over to the offensive. Suave, shrewd, adroit, able, resourceful, he was at one moment coolly and politely insolent and at another deferentially impudent.

At length his strategy was rewarded. Jackson lost his temper, and, most unfortunately, he lost his head at the same time. He appealed to the Tribunal for their ruling that the defendant should be instructed to answer the question put to him with a 'Yes' or a 'No', and not be allowed to digress into political polemics. But the Tribunal ruled against him, whereupon he became petulant, saying that he had better resign and go home. The Tribunal attempted to mollify him and were successful in so far that he withdrew his threat of resignation, but they would not grant him what he asked for and surrendered the continuance of the cross-examination at short notice to David Maxwell Fyfe.

Goering, flushed with triumph, pursued a similar line to that which had had so devastating an effect on Jackson, but David was of a different temperament and calibre. As Francis Biddle later wrote, he 'held on like a bulldog; held on without ever noticing the witness's impertinence, his sallies, his wit and sneers.' Gradually Goering's self-confidence evaporated under David's imperturbable, relentless questioning. He became deflated and defensive; he lost the thread of his argument and contradicted himself. From an arrogant bully he disclosed himself for what he was, a discredited criminal confronted with the proof of his own guilt.

From all accounts – and I have heard many of them – it was a tour de force on the part of David Maxwell Fyfe, a triumph of patience and doggedness comparable to that of Sir Edward Carson during the famous Oscar Wilde trial, when the witness had laughed at him and had been egged on to further witticism by the spectators. Carson had persevered with that same unruffled tenacity until Wilde made his first break ('Did you ever kiss him, Mr Wilde?' 'Oh no, Sir Edward, he was much too ugly'), then Carson struck, pushing Wilde against the wall, stammering and frightened.

It was the same with Maxwell Fyfe and Goering – and I would have given my eye-teeth to have seen it.

David's position at Nuremberg was, in a sense, equivocal. Mr Churchill had entrusted him as Attorney-General with all the preparation on the British side for bringing the Nazi war criminals to justice, and it was in this capacity of chief British prosecutor that he had presided over the International Jurists' Conference, which, during the summer of 1945, had hammered out the details and structure of the International Military Tribunal. Then had come the Conservative defeat at the polls in July and Sir Hartley Shawcross had replaced Maxwell Fyfe as Attorney-General in the Labour Government. The position could have been difficult, but by one of those curious and inexplicable yet eminently sensible accommodations – which are the strength of the British system of government yet incomprehensible to all foreigners – David continued to lead the British prosecution team, as its field commander so to speak, while Hartley came to Nuremberg to make great speeches at the opening and closing of the prosecution's case, but otherwise kept in close contact from London with all that was being done *in situ*. The arrangement worked remarkably well. David's performance at Nuremberg started him upon his distinguished parliamentary career, which led him to the Home Office and later to the Woolsack as Lord Kilmuir. It is a pity that his memoirs are so bitter.

However, to return to my first meeting with the Chief, our conversation began in general terms and we quickly discovered a common interest in Napoleon and in the American Civil War, and also that Stephen McKenna's *Sonia* was among our favourite novels. Then he became more specific. Which of the defendants had I known best? he asked. I told him von Papen and Schacht, and von Neurath whom I had seen a good deal when he was German Ambassador in Rome and in London and also as Foreign Minister. David said that he would like to talk at length with me about all three and then indicated a copy of my *Hindenburg* which lay on his table. 'I always keep it by me,' he said. 'It's invaluable.'

A bell rang a warning that the opening of the morning session was imminent.

'Come along with me,' David said, 'and sit at our table.'

My first glimpse of the court room is engraved indelibly on my memory. It was enormously impressive, quiet, disciplined and judicial. It might have been a British court of justice. On one side of the great hall sat the eight judges forming the International Military Tribunal, one judge and one alternative from each of the four Great Powers, elevated on a dias and wearing black Geneva gowns – except for the Soviet members who had argued with strange logic that since it was called a *Military* Tribunal its members must accordingly be in the guise of soldiers. They had been given the temporary ranks of Major-General and Colonel respectively and wore uniform.

Slightly below them were the officers of the court, prominent among whom was Airey Neave, in his capacity of Marshal. To the right of the Tribunal on the same level and separated by a glass partition were the interpreters. This was one of the first occasions in history when the system of simultaneous multilingual translation was used, and through head-phones and by pressing the appropriate button one could follow the proceedings in English, French, Russian or German. Immediately below the translators, on the floor of the court, stood the witness stand.

To the left of the Tribunal, raised and raked to a high level, was the gallery reserved for the representatives of the press of the world and the V.I.P.s who came from almost as many countries. Beneath these galleries was the entrance to the floor of the court, and here were the tables reserved for the four prosecution teams and their staffs, with their podium a little in advance.

Exactly opposite the Tribunal in a two-tiered dock, the rear wall of which was the door of the lift which communicated with the Prison House, sat the twenty-one defendants, the flower of the Nazi leadership, or what was left of it, for Hitler, Goebbels and Himmler were already dead by their own hands. There sat Goering, Hess, von Ribbentrop, Keitel, Kaltenbrunner, Rosenberg, Frank, Frick, Streicher, Funk, Schacht, Doenitz, Raeder, von Schirach, Sauckel, Jodl, von Papen, Seyss-Inquart, Speer, von Neurath and Fritzsche, charged and indicted with crimes of common conspiracy to commit aggression, crimes against peace, crimes against the laws of war and crimes against humanity.

Originally the accused had numbered twenty-four, but Martin Bormann had never been apprehended and was therefore tried *in absentia*, and before the opening of the trial one of the defendants, Robert Ley, the Labour Front Leader, had committed suicide in his cell, and the aged Gustav Krupp von Bohlen und Halbach had been adjudged too ill and too senile to stand his trial.

Below the dock were the desks of the counsel for the defence who were consistently bobbing up and down to consult their clients. It was not without interest to me to learn that though some of the lawyers involved had prosecuted and some had defended victims of Nazi justice arraigned in the notorious People's Court before the infamous

Roland Freisler, all had rallied, in the best tradition of the German bar, to the defence of the accused.

I recall that my primary reaction on being confronted by this rogues gallery was one of supreme satisfaction. Being of lesser clay I could not share the nobility of Winston Churchill's magnanimity: 'My hatred for them [the Germans] disappeared with their Unconditional Surrender.' I am, I hope and believe, a good friend. I know that I am a 'bonnie hater', and, while I did not entertain a deep-seated loathing for the entire German people – a mental process both senseless and fruitless – I confess to a considerable sense of gratification at seeing these leaders of a tyrannous and foresworn regime brought to book at last.

There in the dock sat those Nazi hierarchs whom I had seen flaunting their arrogance and strutting in their pride during my brief encounter with the Third Reich; there were the high-ranking soldiers and sailors who had betrayed the honour of the officer corps in a mistaken loyalty to a frenzied Führer; there were those men, von Papen and Schacht, who in their conceit had sought to use Hitler and his movement as political hostages and had themselves found that they had caught a tiger by the tail, with the inevitable consequences; there, too, was a Württemberg nobleman, Konstantin von Neurath, who, either through fear of resigning or general lack of moral fortitude, had allowed himself to be sucked more and more deeply into the Nazi morass.

Because of these men, I reflected, millions of combatants and non-combatants had been killed and injured; six million Jews alone had been butchered in cold blood; many men and women in many lands had been murdered and tortured. I thought of my personal friends in the armies of both Britain and Germany who had died on the field of battle or had been grievously wounded, and of my German friends who had languished in exile or, worse still, had died miserably and in inhuman circumstances because of their courage in resisting Hitler. Lastly, it occurred to me that, but for the grace of God, I, if these villains had had their way on the bloody Night of the Long Knives, as I have described in *Knaves, Fools and Heroes*, would almost certainly not be looking at them now from 'the other side of the fence'.

I realised I lacked that legal detachment which becomes a great jurist. Because of all these crimes, I felt no pity for these men who were now called to answer for their offences against humanity. I gazed at them with the deepest attention, and it was interesting to me and to others present that my appearance at the prosecution table caused a ripple of recognition in the dock, and that some of the prisoners conferred with their lawyers.

To work with David Maxwell Fyfe was an education in itself. It has always delighted me to watch a brilliant mind in action and now I had the opportunity of doing so at close quarters.

We usually had our sessions together at lunchtime, eating off trays at either side of his desk, and he would ask me simply to talk to him of the three defendants in whose prosecution he thought I could help him – von Papen, Schacht and von Neurath. I told him all I knew, and the most minute details returned to my mind as I talked. He would sit silently, drinking it all in, now asking an appropriate question, now making a single note, now quoting some passage from my *Hindenburg* on which he needed further elucidation.

David prepared his cross-examination with meticulous care and precisely drawn diagrams indicating the alternative lines on which his interrogation would proceed according to which answer he received to a previous question. It was in the course of these questionings that one could descry the items of information that one had given him and the astonishingly pertinent use which he made of them in conjunction with his documents. Often he would catch the defendant off his guard with an intimate detail or a revealing reference. It was always a dazzling performance and I would sit, breathless and on the edge of my chair, waiting to hear what was coming next, what trap was being set for an unwary witness.

Indeed, one of the most interesting aspects of being in the position of half-observer, half-participant, was to watch the difference in the *modi operandi* of the diverse national techniques of cross-examination. The British were the most varied. Together with David's combination of silk and steel went Harry Phillimore's impervious blandness concealing a hidden lightning thrust, and added to these was the ruthless, almost brutal, technique of 'Khaki' Roberts as he hacked down his victims like a hatchet man. Elwyn Jones's lilting Welsh voice was deceptive but lethal, while Mervyn Griffith-Jones was calm and effective.

The Americans, to a man, were more dramatic. From Bob Jackson downwards there was a hint of the Hollywood technique – 'Answer me yes or no' – which sometimes came off but, as in the example of Jackson versus Goering, could fail lamentably. But with some defendants it proved more successful than the suaver methods of the British.

The French were a disappointment to me. Reared on the legend of Maître Labori's histrionic interpellation in the Dreyfus case, I had expected fireworks. Their process was, also, pedestrian and there seemed to be a lack of fire in their performance.

If the French were dull, however, all lack of entertainment was made up for by the Russians. General Rudenko and his colleagues, also disguised as soldiers, employed a system all their own. They moved to the attack like a clanking armoured column, relying on intimidation for the principal results.

'Now, defendant,' Rudenko would demand of some wretched figure on the witness stand, 'have you read the document which I have just presented to you?' The witness would admit that he had. 'And do you admit that it is your signature upon it?' 'Yes,' the victim would reply. 'And do you now confess that you are a Fascist beast?' Rudenko would thunder. Sometimes a defendant would have sufficient courage to deny this charge, whereupon Rudenko would drop his voice to a melodramatic stage whisper. 'Very well,' he would hiss, 'the Tribunal will know how to judge by your answer. I will now proceed to my next question.'

Between them, however, the four teams produced a damning indictment of the accused. They exposed to the horrified world a pageant of infamy and brutality, of 'man's inhumanity to man' and of man's capacity for dishonour and perfidy that was to make the name of the Third Reich a stench in the nostrils of the civilised world and a stigma which will remain for generations. A 'Procession of Protracted Death', it was a withering away of the very soul of Germany. Names such as Belsen and Auschwitz, Buchenwald and Ravensbrück and Dachau, flamed across the court room; crimes of genocide and of wholesale slavery, such as had been unknown in Europe since the Middle Ages, were bared to view. Those present in Court were often physically sickened by the bestial details of atrocities and appalled by the evidence of betrayal of a nation's pledged word.

All this had emerged from examination, cross-examination and the use of documents, most of official German origin, and the process of their emergence had been conducted in the cold, relentless, but eminently detached atmosphere of a court of justice. None of the accused nor their defending counsel at any point questioned the fairness of the Nuremberg proceedings.

Many of them had known other trials under other circumstances. Among my Nuremberg memories one of the most dramatic is of the film of the People's Court in Berlin trying those who had been implicated in the plot to assassinate Hitler on 20 July 1944.

This film had been among the mass of official German documentary material which had fallen into Allied hands and on which the prosecution had based its case. There had been a second part for which we had searched diligently but without success. It had been made at Hitler's express orders for his own delectation, and had shown the executions of the wretched men, slowly strangled by thin wire hanging naked from a meat-hook. This second part had been intended for select audiences among the military, but its effect had been so greatly the opposite of what had been expected that every copy had been destroyed on the direct order of Goebbels; I have in my posession, however, copies of the affidavits of the cinema operator who took the film and of the prison guard who watched him do it. The record of the proceedings of the People's Court proved quite sufficient.

The Court had been darkened, and a screen hung down before the translators' box. The film showed in agonising horror the degree to which public humiliation could be used to undermine the morale of an accused person. No means had been unexploited to reduce the accused to the lowest depths of ignominy. Their false teeth, their belts, their braces had been taken from them and they appeared unkempt and unshaven. Moreover the behaviour of the Judge, Roland Freisler, was a disgrace, a subject of disgust. Even as we listened our ears were offended by the venomous clangour of his voice which bore down before it all the half-hearted attempts of the accused to refute the charges.

'You dirty old man, why do you keep fiddling with your trousers?' Freisler screamed at von Witzleben as, toothless and mumbling, the ex-Field-Marshal desperately clutched at his waist to escape indignity; and when another former general objected to being called a *Schweinehund*, the Presiding Judge asked if he could suggest a more suitable animal. 'You are a filthy rascal,' he shouted at another of the accused. 'You are merely a little pile of shit which has lost all self-respect.'

On and on went the storm of abuse which had been Nazi justice but at last this terrifying film came to an end. The lights went on. The occupants of the dock appeared white and shaken; some of them wiped sweat from their brows. There was a deathly silence broken at length by the calm, judicial voice of Lord Justice Lawrence, President of the Tribunal, 'We will now proceed with the case in hand.'

The contrast was complete.

Of course we had lighter moments. The prolonged tension of the trial would have been insupportable if we could not have found something to laugh at occasionally.

Lord Justice Lawrence, the senior British member of the Tribunal, had established a unique reputation at Nuremberg. It had been the original intention that the Presidency of the Tribunal should go by rota among the four senior Judges, each occupying the chair for a month. Sir Geoffrey Lawrence was the first occupant and at the close of this period so admirably had he discharged his office that his colleagues unanimously elected him their permanent President. Throughout the long months of the trial he gave to the proceedings much of its decorum, its wisdom and its impartiality.

His personal dignity was proof against any emergency. One warm August afternoon, in the somnolent air of a post-luncheon session, he had dozed behind his hand as has many another great legal luminary under similar circumstances. In the witness box was an S.S. officer who was being examined by defence counsel on behalf of that organisation. The witness was at pains to deny the existence of horrors in concentration camps, in which, he said, the aim was to give the inmates a life 'worthy of human beings'. Every facility was afforded them. 'They had,' said the S.S. man, 'regular mail service. They had a large camp library, even books in foreign languages. They had variety shows, motion pictures, sporting contests. They even had a bordello.' At this moment Sir Geoffrey Lawrence came to full consciousness. With grave interest he asked the witness, 'What was it they even had?' His friend and American colleague Francis Biddle sought to enlighten him. 'Brothels,' he interpolated, not realising that the public announcement system on the bench was live. 'What did he say?' asked the now thoroughly aroused President. 'Bordello, whore-house,' thundered Judge Biddle, and suddenly noticed from the rising tide of amusement in the court-room that they were overheard. 'I see,' said Sir Geoffrey, with immense dignity. 'The witness may proceed.'

It was in the course of the hearing of this same defence in the case against the S.S. that my own sometimes warped sense of humour brought me to the brink of disaster. We had listened for a very long time to a series of character-witnesses who had testified with monotonous uniformity to the fine and virtuous nature of the essential attributes demanded of candidates for membership in Himmler's élite corps. They must be perfect physical specimens, sound in wind and limb, excelling in athletics, yet having intellectual attainments of high quality and impeccable personal characters. It was represented to us that these were super-men, outstanding examples to those 'lesser breeds without the law', leaders and paladins in every sense.

It seemed to me that I had come across a similar catalogue of virtues in other circumstances and I suddenly realised what those circumstances had been. It would have been better and wiser had I been satisfied with keeping this discovery to myself, but I was moved to share it. I wrote on a piece of paper, 'They might all qualify as Rhodes Scholars,' and passed it to David Maxwell Fyfe. For some reason it touched his sense of risibility and I saw him make a superhuman effort and control his emotions. At the close of the session he sent for me and gave me a magisterial dressing-down. 'If you try to make me laugh in court again,' said he, 'I'll send you home by the next plane.'

The incident seemed to have remained in his mind, however, because years later, when as Visitor he came to St Antony's College, of which I was a founding Fellow, he made reference to it in his postprandial remarks at a gaudy.

Francis Biddle was an inveterate chatterer on the bench, and one evening he returned to us at the villa in high delight at an exchange he had had with Norman Birkett. It so happened that Doctor George Boehm, one of the defence counsel for the S.S., had, in the course of his argument, said, 'They were not even allowed any official party intercourse.' This was too much for Francis's ever bubbling sense of humour and he passed a note to Birkett: 'Do you feel like a little official party intercourse, old thing?' Back came the impromptu answer from Birkett's piquant pen:

> Intercourse with Party Members
>   Sounds alluring when it's said.
> Every man, of course, remembers
>   Golden moments spent in bed;
> But the thought persists and vexes
>   'Is that quite the thing it seems?'
> Intercourse for both the sexes
>   Sounds too much like party dreams.

The most exciting form of relaxation, however, and one not entirely free from danger, was the sporting proclivities of Geoffrey Lawrence. He loved to shoot. It was his favourite Sunday ploy to organise a rough shoot and to enlist the services of his friends and colleagues as beaters.

On the only occasion I participated in one of these *battues* I went out with Pat Dean. We met Geoffrey Lawrence at a field of kale which sloped gently upwards to a small eminence. Now, great jurist though he was, gallant and dashing gunner officer though he had been in the First World War, our President of the Tribunal could not be said to be a superlatively good shot, and, as a beater, I was not without trepidation. Taking his stand at the top of the hillock he gave us the signal to advance, which we did, driving all sorts of birds and beasts uphill before us. Geoffrey

48

Lawrence loosed off pretty indiscriminately and as we drew nearer the risk became perceptibly greater.

Pat was considerably braver than I was and strode forward with the determination of the Old Guard at Waterloo; as for me, I was among those *grognards* who 'grumbled but followed'. I am not aware that any casualties actually occurred, but I also discovered that I was not alone in my apprehension. At least it took one's mind off the sordid details of the trial.

By the end of August the evidence for and against the accused had been concluded, as had the processes of direct and cross-examination. The last memorable speeches had been delivered and the Tribunal adjourned to give the members time to consider their judgement and decide their sentences. I returned to Ruth and to Garsington, and we passed an agreeable month catching up on all that had happened during my absence, seeing our friends and enjoying the country and London.

Saturday, 28 September, found me back at Nuremberg, where Rebecca West and I were again the guests of Francis Biddle. The Tribunal was to begin the reading of its judgement on Monday the thirtieth, and on the Sunday we drove for lunch to Bamberg, that beautiful baroque Bavarian town, which had mercifully come through the war unscathed. We visited the Cathedral and admired the famous statue of the Bamberger Reiter, whom the ill-fated Claus von Stauffenberg was supposed to resemble. It was a delicious autumn day of warmth and peace and sunshine.

That evening the Tribunal dined together and met afterwards in informal session. We had been joined at the villa by Francis Biddle's cousin Tony with his pretty new Canadian bride, who had come to see the closing act of the drama. Tony Biddle had been American Ambassador in Warsaw at the outbreak of war, and had shared the danger and hardships of the Polish Government in its retreat to Rumania

and subsequently to France, where they were housed at
Angers until evacuated once again to London in 1940. Later
he had been accredited to all the governments-in-exile resi-
dent in London. He was charming, handsome and amusing
but something of a lightweight.

Francis Biddle returned home very late that night and
obviously in some perturbation. Rebecca and I had sat up
for him but all he would say was, 'Something very unpleasant
has happened. The Russians have let us down. I can say no
more now.'

Next morning, the Tribunal reassembled in plenary session
and its members began to read in turn the text of their
judgement. It took all day and part of the next, but before
he left after breakfast on the second day Francis Biddle said
Delphically to me, 'I'm afraid you're in for a disappointment.'

1 October 1946 was the last day of the Nuremberg Trials
– the day of reckoning. It had lasted nearly eleven months
during which the accused had listened to the testimony of
their crimes. Some had behaved with great dignity; some had
blustered; some had wept, others admitted their guilt; nearly
all had lied. Now the hour of Nemesis was approaching,
and for the last time as a group the accused sat in the dock
to hear judgement and verdict.

I do not think that anyone who was present on that
occasion can ever forget the experience. There was an elec-
tric tension throughout the court-room, palpable alike in
the body of the court, in the press seats and in the visitors'
gallery which was crowded with distinguished persons as
never before since the beginning of the trials. The suppressed
excitement extended even to the tables of the prosecution
where, behind a mask of professional impassivity, all waited
with anxiety and suspense to hear the results of their great
indictment. The Tribunal concluded the delivery of its
judgement before rendering its verdict and sentences. It was
for these that we all waited.

I was now to understand the meaning of Francis Biddle's

cryptic warning of disappointment. The Tribunal found all
the accused guilty, with the exception of Schacht von
Papen and Fritzsche, who were acquitted and discharged
from the Court. Of these verdicts Fritzsche's was almost a
foregone conclusion for he had been but a pale shadow of
his master, Goebbels. The acquittal of Schacht, however,
and of von Papen sent a momentary wave of incredulous
surprise over the court-room after the announcement of each
verdict. There was, of course, no audible discussion, but it
was as if the collective shock which many present, of whom
I was most certainly one, had sustained manifested itself
in an almost visible manner. Von Papen gave his habitual
vulpine grin – the Silver Fox had once again given the hounds
the slip. Schacht, the picture of smug complacency, had
never doubted the verdict for a moment. Had he not cynically
affirmed to Airey Neave, when the latter had served the
indictment upon him, that 'You can't hang a banker'?

The reading of the verdicts ended and the court adjourned
for lunch. In the dock there was an unwonted stir and conversation. The defendants were about to separate for the last
time, and before they passed one by one into the steel lift
which communicated with the cells they spoke together
for a moment. The three acquitted men received the con-
gratulations of their counsel and in some cases of their
co-defendants. Schacht received a number of handshakes,
but none from Goering, and a few minutes later was auction-
ing his autograph for bars of chocolate in the court-house
canteen. Fritzsche received somewhat perfunctory con-
gratulations. No one, save his counsel and his son, shook
hands with von Papen.

When the Tribunal reconvened for the final afternoon
session, they confronted for the first time in eleven months
an empty dock. The eighteen remaining defendants must
now appear one by one to hear their doom. There was an
awed hush, a constrained silence, in the court-room as we
waited; a silence broken at length by the sound of the

opening of the back panel of the dock and Goering, standing between two guards, appeared framed in the dark aperture. I noticed that for some reason, whereas his hands were free, all the subsequent defendants were handcuffed.

In the next twenty minutes we heard eleven men individually condemned to death – Goering, Ribbentrop, Keitel, Kaltenbrunner, Rosenberg, Frank, Frick, Streicher, Sauckel, Jodl and Seyss-Inquart. The atmosphere within the court had grown tense and almost ghoulish. No one of those present had listened before to such a mass condemnation to the ultimate penalty, and it was virtually with relief that we heard Lord Justice Lawrence sentence Doenitz to ten years' imprisonment, Funk, Raeder and Hess to imprisonment for life and Baldur von Schirach to twenty years. Then followed sentences on Speer for twenty years and von Neurath for fifteen years, and then the death sentence on the absent Bormann pronounced to an empty dock brought the grim succession to a close.

In the moment of hushed silence which followed the pronouncement of the last sentence, it was as if there echoed through the court-room the last eloquent appeal of Sir Hartley Shawcross in his closing address for the prosecution: 'These are our laws – let them prevail.' The judgement of the civilised world had been visited upon those who had dared, in the full knowledge of the penalty of failure, to attempt the substitution of the reign of terror for the reign of law. It was a moment in which one hoped for – and almost glimpsed – a new order in which the solidarity of comradeship among the Four Powers who had dealt out justice at Nuremberg should lead the suffering, yearning peoples of the world to a happier way of life.

But all prospect of the realisation of this vision, together with that fine display of quadripartite solidarity and co-operation which had been so salient and inspiring a characteristic of the trial, was shattered by the closing statement of Sir Geoffrey Lawrence. 'I have an announcement to make,' he said in those grave tones that had not lost their firm dignity throughout the trial. He made known to us that the Soviet member of the Tribunal had recorded his dissent from the three acquittals and was of the opinion that Hess should have received a death sentence. In addition he was of the opinion that the Reich Cabinet and the General Staff and High Command should have been declared to be criminal organisations along with the Leadership Corps, the Gestapo, the S.D. and the S.S.

As we passed out of the shadow of the court-house into the crisp sunlit October air, much of the sense of achievement had departed, to be replaced by infinite sadness.

Rebecca West and I returned to Francis Biddle's villa in a dejected frame of mind. The Tony Biddles had departed but Hartley Shawcross dined with us that night, and Francis talked to us about the trial as he had not felt free to do before. To my enquiry as to why it had been necessary to acquit von Papen and Schacht, for whom I had hoped that prison sentences would be forthcoming, he replied that, although they were obviously evil men, and that this had been clear in the text of the judgement, they had been guilty only of assisting Hitler to come to power. This was not a crime within the terms of the Charter of the Tribunal who had therefore no choice but to acquit them as they were innocent of the various charges under the indictment.

He then told us the background of the Soviet caveats. It would appear that in the course of their deliberations after the adjournment in August the Judges had arrived at complete unanimity in regard to their judgement, their verdicts and the sentences which were to be imposed. They also agreed not to communicate these facts to their governments in advance, thereby indicating complete independence. On the night of 29 September, as we knew, the Tribunal had held an informal meeting, and after its conclusion General Nikichenko had come to Francis Biddle and, in evident distress and regret, had confessed that at the last moment his courage had failed him and that he had communicated the text of the Tribunal's judgement to Moscow, with the result that imperative orders had arrived from the Kremlin for him to make formal dissent from certain of the decisions on which he and his colleagues had reached a unanimous decision. Francis, greatly upset, had told him that he must go at once to Geoffrey Lawrence and inform him of this new development; on no account must it be sprung upon the Tribunal as a surprise. It was after this that he had returned home in the state of perturbation evident to Rebecca West and myself. So much, one thought, for Soviet justice.

It was a fortnight later, on 15 October, that the world was startled by Goering's last triumphantly arrogant gesture of suicide, and on the following day the remaining ten under sentence of death were hanged in the jail at Nuremberg. I had received and had refused an invitation to attend the executions and, though I should not have considered doing so under any circumstances, I was particularly glad not to be a witness of what proved to be an intolerably bungled affair. The British Government had offered the services of the official hangman, Pierrepoint, for this purpose but the offer had been declined and the episode had been marred by a singular inefficiency of performance on the part of those who were in charge of it.

Shortly afterwards, however, I did take the opportunity of visiting the jail at Spandau in the British sector of Berlin, to which the six who had been sentenced to imprisonment had been removed. I lunched with the Commandants of the guard who were responsible for the security of the prisoners and was permitted to see them at exercise. Spandau jail had been built to house six hundred criminals; it was now given over to the six remaining leaders of Hitler's Thousand-Year Reich. Of the half-dozen whom I saw on that November afternoon all have either died or have completed their sentences. All, that is to say, save one. Due entirely to the implacable and indefensible bloody-mindedness of the Soviet government, the octogenarian Rudolf Hess remains the sole occupant of Spandau jail.

Before the close of 1946 Pat Dean's period of service as a temporary civil servant terminated, and he departed from the Legal Department of the Foreign Office where he had served with distinction throughout the war. He was sad about this as he had enjoyed his association with the Office, but both he and I were pleased and gratified when it was proposed that we should together write the official history of the Nuremberg Trials. This suggestion came jointly from the Foreign Secretary, Ernie Bevin, and the Attorney-General, Hartley Shawcross, and it was understood that the book would appear under their combined patronage.

We accepted and in due course received our letters of appointment signed by our two august patrons, with whom we had several interviews. We were a sound complementary choice. Pat had the legal experience and knowledge and I the historical expertise. Moreover we liked one another and the prospect of working together was agreeable to both of us.

We began at once to plan the scope and nature of the book and had even got some early chapters drafted when disaster overtook the project. Moley Sargent, Permanent Under-Secretary of the Foreign Office, was dismayed at being deprived of the services of Pat Dean (whom he had regarded as one of the best and most reliable German experts in the Service), and with unwonted alacrity he took action to remedy the loss. Within six months of leaving the Legal Department Pat was back on the permanent strength as head of the newly-formed German Department, his feet thus set upon the ladder of a distinguished diplomatic career, which, besides service in London, led him to Rome, New York and Washington.

This precipitate action of Moley's, though doubtless justified by results and displaying both courage and imagination, left me holding the baby. What had been intended as a joint complementary authorship had now been shorn of one of its vital parts, and I was totally deficient of the legal knowledge which Pat was to have provided. In desperation I attempted the fatal task of reasoning with Moley, who, though a very good friend, was totally uninterested in an official history of the Nuremberg trials. 'What am I to do,' I asked, 'now that you've taken Pat Dean away from me?' Moley was at his blandest, his most facetiously disarming best. 'I don't understand you, my dear Jack,' he replied. 'I haven't taken Pat away from you at all. You are perfectly welcome to his partnership during the week-ends.'

To this there was little to say. I tried for some time to find some international lawyer who could spare the time to help me, but without success. Alas, the Official History of the Nuremberg Trials has never been written.

My curious association with Franz von Papen did not, however, close with Nuremberg. Although acquitted by the International Military Tribunal, he had a hard time ahead of him at the hands of his fellow countrymen. As a result of the de-nazification proceedings brought against him he received a jail sentence in the course of which he was kicked in the jaw by a contumacious fellow-prisoner who had been an S.S. man. However, that incredible capacity for survival, which had delivered him alike from Nazi violence and international justice, now carried him to some progressive degree of rehabilitation, so that within a few years he was a familiar figure on the race tracks of Western Germany.

Moreover he wrote his memoirs, which were published in London in 1952, where they achieved not a little success. 'I wondered why he published it first in England,' wrote Heinrich Brüning to me from America on 6 August – displaying a satirical sense of humour with which he was too rarely credited – 'and conclude that he did it from resentment against you. To accuse a Düsseldorf Uhlan officer of "brushing his fences" ' (I had written this in *Hindenburg*) 'was, of course, unpardonable! Had you said the same about an Uhlan officer of the Guards, he might have been only amused by it.'

I reviewed the book anonymously and with some acerbity, for 'Franchen's' memoirs were remarkable more for their mendacity than their historical value. On 2 December 1952, Brüning (in a letter from Cologne, signed 'Harry') sent me the following comment: 'I read the review of Papen's book and congratulate the reviewer, about whose identity there was no doubt for me after reading certain sentences. But I keep strictly to the tradition of the *Literary Supplement* in not mentioning his name. But I want to congratulate him.'

I had the last word on von Papen, however. I had the satisfaction of writing his obituary.

It had been hoped by many of us, in those wishful days of 1946, that the experiment of the International Military Tribunal would pave the way for some permanent Court of International Criminal Justice to be established as part of the machinery of the United Nations, together with an International Criminal Code embracing the Nuremberg Principles. Efforts towards this end were indeed made by President Truman, Francis Biddle and Trygve Lie, the Secretary-General of the United Nations. As a result of these the Assembly did adopt a resolution, in December 1946, affirming the Nuremberg Principles of International Law, and, after endless delays, a draft statute for an International Criminal Court was presented to the Assembly in 1953. More than twenty years later, so far as I am aware, the statute still remains only a draft.

So the present position of the Nuremberg Trials is that they occupy an outstanding place in international legal history and no more than that. In some degree, however, they do justify the saying that 'Civilisation does get forward, sometimes upon a powder cart.' Personally I regret nothing of the process, believing it to have been essential, honourable and, indeed, inevitable. As it stands, however, in its isolated distinction, it creates a not entirely happy precedent. I once remarked to Bruce Lockhart, as he records, 'Next time the right side may not win.'

CHAPTER THREE

The Bare Bones of History

When I was a young and budding historian I had 'a thing' about documents. I believed that in documents lay the real truth of history and I used to have wonderful dreams of being given the free run of the Green Registry of the Foreign Office, finding therein the answers to all the problems which had perplexed me in my studies.

I was soon to lose my naïve beliefs, but never my basic interest, in documents, which have justifiably been described as the 'bare bones of history'. What I have discovered, however, is that historical truth – in that it exists at all – lies not in documents alone, nor in memoirs, diaries, biographies or oral history. All these are essential and invaluable factors in the historian's armoury but, when the chips are down, the final result depends on the historian himself alone, on his ability to weigh, assay and analyse the accumulated material at his disposal and to come up with his own honest opinions and conclusions. There are no answers at the back of the book.

The essential danger, the basic menace to the attainment of historical truth, is the inevitability of rationalisation, the wholly understandable desire in all of us to appear at our best under the scalpel of historical dissection, and are we not all prone to the use of either exaggeration or palliation in our own interests? To this end some have succumbed to the temptation of *suppressio veri* and even to that of *suggestio falsi*. There are also certain memoirs, such as those of Prince Bülow, which are deliberate studies in historical mendacity and – on the other side of the picture – memoirs such as Heinrich Brüning's, which succeed in presenting a far less favourable impression of the author than is justified or accurate.

One value of the use of documents lies in that through them it is often possible to correct misrepresentations, whether intentional or fortuitous. On the other hand they may be seen to be palpably contradictory. Now that the national archives of so many countries have been made accessible to students it is all too easy to read both sides of the same conversation – sometimes with surprising results.

Suppose, for example, the Graustark ambassador in Strelsau is instructed by his government to make strong representation to the Ruritanian foreign minister on some issue that has been for some time a sore point between them. The ambassador calls at the ministry for foreign affairs and presents a note, the general gist of which he has communicated in advance. He develops the point of view of Graustark with polite vehemence, to which the foreign minister replies with equally courteous obstinacy that the Ruritanian government is unable to depart from the position which it has taken up. At the close of a sharp rally, which concludes with 'love all', the ambassador takes his leave with an impeccable degree of disagreement equalled only by the flawlessly expressed reiteration on the part of the foreign minister.

All in all one would have thought that it was a case of 'honours even', but this is frequently not borne out by the documents. As he drives back to his embassy the representative of Graustark is struck by the compelling and unanswerable arguments which he might have made in his exchanges with his Ruritanian opposite number, and these pearls of diplomatic wit conceivably may find their way eventually into the despatch which he sends to his chief. Equally, luxuriating in his bath before dinner, the Ruritanian foreign minister is suddenly aware of a brilliant riposte with which he might have demolished the case of his troublesome visitor, and, in due course, this may be incorporated in the memorandum which he will later prepare for the enlightenment of his cabinet colleagues.

It is not unknown for both sides to claim to have gained a tactical victory in this manner and the unfortunate searcher after truth must suffer accordingly and, since faced with a situation which is manifestly impossible, will be compelled to fall back upon his own instincts and power of interpretation. I myself have often longed to find in some musty archive a despatch which contained the welcome admission: 'At this point in the discussion I confess I was punch-drunk and hanging on the ropes.' I would believe the writer implicitly.

I would not for the world, however, deny the importance of documents in the resources of the historian. All that I would warn against is the belief that the immortal and everlasting truth is to be found in the use of documents alone.

A primary issue in the field of documentary research is that you can find the papers. The British Government, or more explicitly the Foreign Office and the Cabinet Office, have over the years been most understandably reluctant to give up custody of papers, which, though they might not involve the security of the realm, contained secrets of intimate discussions and important issues of which these departments were the guardians. For years the 'fifty-year rule' was regarded as sacrosanct, that is to say no official document could be consulted – except under special and rare circumstances – until it was fifty years old. After the conclusion of the Second World War a strong lobby of historians began to agitate for a relaxation of this restriction, a course of action that was firmly resisted in Whitehall. A prolonged confrontation ensued at the conclusion of which it was conceded that, with certain essential safeguards, the fifty-year rule should be reduced to a thirty-year rule made operative as from 1 January 1968.

By way of an additional *douceur*, a further concession opened the documents specifically affecting the course of the war for the full period of the war years, that is to say until September 1945. It is therefore possible, for example, to consult the Cabinet minutes from the date of their initiation by Lloyd George in 1917 until the close of the Japanese War – and devilishly dull reading much of them make.

As a historian I can appreciate the arguments on both sides. Their range runs from the one extreme of 'Let the people know' to the other, which is epitomised by Arthur Balfour's expressed preference for 'open treaties secretly arrived at'. I share the delight and the hunger of all my fellows at the opening up of this rich new field of material, and yet I am not absolutely happy about the ultimate results.

The item of highest value in any file or dossier is, of course, the original document itself, but very often the juiciest morsels for the historian are to be found in the minutes which accompany it. The essential significance of these minutes lies in the absolute freedom of thought and expression in the mind of the writer. If his opinion is to be worth its while to his chief in making up his mind, he must feel at liberty to state his sincere agreement or disagreement with the original document. Now, thirty years is not a very long time. When these minutes are placed in the public domain under the new act, many of the younger men and women who have thus expressed themselves will still be alive and they may well be perturbed at the prospect of having their remarks, made in confidence in the light of the circumstances as they were then known, made public to the critical gaze of scholars who, with the wisdom of hindsight, may well take issue with their opinions and their judgements. My fear is that with this alarming prospect looming over their shoulders, civil servants may be tempted to hedge in the frankness of their minutes and the freedom of their opinions. This in its turn may well diminish the value of the archives to the researches of future historians, and a sort of law of diminishing returns may well ensue. This is worth thinking about.

As for me, I made my entry into the bastion of documentary history through the German rather than the British portal, first at Nuremberg and later in a more official capacity.

In the final months of the war a haul of some four hundred tons of German Foreign Ministry documents fell into the hands of units of the U.S. First Army in the Harz Mountain area. The reason for the discovery of this treasure trove was due in large measure to the incomplete execution of orders from Berlin to destroy the most important portions of the archives, and also to a lack of understanding on the part of those who issued those orders of the professional psychology of archivists, who would rather eviscerate their own children than destroy the material entrusted to their charge.

By 1943 the attacks of the British and American air forces on German cities became intensified with the result that the Reich government began the dispersal of its archives from Berlin. A skeleton staff and the current files of the Foreign Ministry were retained in the Wilhelmstrasse; the remainder with the bulk of the documents were moved to Krümmhubel, a resort in the Riesengebirge region, but some were sent as far distant as Lake Constance on the Swiss frontier. Some were also despatched to castles in the Harz Mountains and to locations south and east of Berlin. In the summer and autumn of 1944 these latter *caches* became threatened by the westward sweep of the Red Army and their contents were concentrated in the Harz. By 1945 nearly the whole of the Foreign Ministry archives had been concentrated in the west.

Early in April orders were issued for progressive destruction, including all important files of the Nazi period. This, however, was asking more than archival flesh and blood could bear. Files were intended by God to be cherished not destroyed. In the words of the immortal Marie Lloyd, 'they dillied and they dallied', so that when units of General Courtney Hodges's U.S. First Army entered the Harz Mountain region later in the month only the barest minimum of destruction had been effected – just sufficient, in fact, to strike a nice balance between the dominant conscience of the archivist and the inborn obedience of the German bureaucrat. Interrogation of these men, plus additional documentary evidence captured later, disposed of the suspicion which had naturally lurked in our minds, that the archives had been purposely planted by the Nazis in the path of the victorious Anglo-American armies, and that spurious documents had been added to the collection with the purpose of sowing discord among Germany's enemies. This, it was decided, though a reasonable possibility, was not the case.

The chance of finding such a precious haul of material had not been overlooked by the Western Powers, and teams of Anglo-American experts were being held in readiness. These now descended upon the newly liberated areas and, in addition to those already lovingly surrendered by their custodians, further discoveries were made in the Harz region and in Thuringia. All these treasures were now assembled at the Schloss in Marburg, a university town in the American zone, where Franz von Papen had made his not uncourageous appeal to the German people which had triggered off the Night of the Long Knives on 20 June 1934. Here the mass of material was sorted and analysed by the Anglo-American experts with highly successful results, their most important find being a box containing memoranda summarising conversations between Hitler and Ribbentrop with foreign statesmen.

Documents, however, were not the only fish which fetched up in our net at Marburg. The organisation of the Schloss was an Anglo-American enterprise, and the chief administrative officer was a most admirable British sergeant-major, whose

efficiency and imperturbability in the face of emergency became proverbial. Yet even his marmoreal calm was somewhat shaken on one occasion.

It was a dark and stormy night when an American army
truck, driven by a wet and dispirited G.I., drove up to the
entrance of the Schloss. The boy deposited three sizeable
packing-cases in the hall. He had, he said, found them in
a German truck abandoned by the side of the road and
having received somewhat vague instructions to bring all
unusual finds to the Schloss he had done so. He demanded
a receipt and drove off again into the night.

Our sergeant-major was naturally used to receiving strange
packages, most of which contained archival material, and
he gave orders for the cases to be opened, but even his
British phlegm was scarcely proof against the contents
revealed. There on the floor of the hall lay three coffins in
good condition. But they were no ordinary coffins, for upon
each was a gold plate proclaiming them to contain the
remains of Frederick the Great, President Field-Marshal von
Hindenburg and his wife.

It was subsequently discovered that the Hindenburgs, who
had originally been interred in a great mausoleum on the
battlefield of Tannenberg, had been removed during the
retreat of the Wehrmacht across East Prussia before the
advance of the Red Army, and had been brought to Berlin.
Thence they had been again evacuated westwards to prevent
their falling into the profaning hands of the Russians, and
this time they were accompanied by Frederick the Great,
who had been exhumed from his tomb in the Garrison
Church at Potsdam, over which, ironically enough, Hindenburg and Hitler had been photographed in their famous
handshake some twelve years before. Now they lay together
in even stranger surroundings.

The disposal of these relics initially presented something
of a problem to the British and American authorities, but
it was resolved in a civilised and sophisticated manner. The

Field-Marshal and his wife were given a dignified burial in a side chapel of the Cathedral of Marburg, which is a thing of austere beauty. Frederick the Great offered more of a difficulty, but this too was suitably and properly settled by handing his coffin over to the present head of the House of Hohenzollern, my friend Prince Louis Ferdinand of Prussia, who gave it repose in the family castle of Hechingen, in the Duchy of Hohenzollern, south of Württemberg.

The first purpose to which this documentary trove was put was in connection with the Nuremberg Trials. As I have written in the previous chapter, all charges included in the indictment (with the one infamous exception of the Katyn massacre) were based upon the official archives of the Germans themselves, and not the least impressive aspect of the proceedings of the International Military Tribunal was the extent to which the Nazi leaders were convicted on the evidence of their own documents. To achieve this, teams of experts attached to the British and American prosecution staffs had examined thousands of papers which they had assembled into the massive Nuremberg archive. They were made publicly accessible at the conclusion of the trials and of the forty-two volumes of the proceedings seventeen are devoted to documents.

This 'fringe benefit' of the Nuremberg Trials constitutes an inestimable boon to students of the history of the inter-war and war years. It is as if the cream of the secret registries of Whitehall had suddenly been thrown open to scholars – without the restriction of even the thirty-year rule! Without the circumstances of the trials this could never have happened. The proceedings of the International Military Tribunal gave to historians what more than a quarter of a century of research could not have accomplished.

There is a school of thought among historians in Britain, in America and in Germany who jeer at the Nuremberg documentation, who throw doubt upon its validity and who

65

warn others of our calling against the danger of using it. Among their principal targets is the famous Hossbach Protocol, which represents the record of Hitler's notorious 'blueprint for aggression' which he outlined to his chief lieutenants on 5 November 1937.

With this school of thought, as with that of the New Left in respect of the cold war, I must respectfully disagree. The Hossbach Protocol stands, to my mind, firmly on its own feet, but there is also plenty of supporting evidence. Its critics must presumably know, for example, though I have never seen it quoted by them, a memorandum written by Hitler to Schacht in September 1936 (more than a year *before* the events recorded in the Hossbach Protocol) embodying his decision to override all objections from Schacht and his fellow economists and financiers to make Germany as self-sufficient as possible and to have both the German army and the German economy ready for war in four years time (that is, by 1940).

Historians of the period will naturally apply to the Nuremberg documentation those acid tests of scholarship which are essential in the use and evaluation of all such material. For me the most important aspect of this issue lies in the fact that, thanks to the existence of the International Military Tribunal, *we have the documentation to which to apply the tests.* That is all that is claimed for them and it is sufficient. They provide one of the most important contributions to source material in this century.

The Nuremberg documentation was, however, only a segment of the archival hoard at Marburg. Here the Foreign Ministry files were being augmented almost daily by the uncovering or surrender of further collections. These accretions included many tons of Chancellery documents and the Schloss seemed bulging at the seams.

It had been a fundamental principle of policy among the allied powers that the German people should be convinced irrefutably of the causes, the magnitude and the consequences of their defeat. There must be no danger of the repetition of the mistakes made at the conclusion of the First World War when this impression was never fully brought home to Germany. Unconditional surrender, the assumption of German sovereignty by the four powers and the total occupation of the country provided pretty convincing evidence of the magnitude of defeat, but there remained the causes and the consequences.

These had occupied many hours of the discussions on the sub-committees of the European Advisory Commission, of which I was a member of the British delegation, and many memoranda of guidance had been prepared for the eradication from the German mentality of that particular kink, that *furor teutonicus*, which evokes such evils as those of National Socialism and the ferocity of Prussian militarism. These early thoughts of the E.A.C. eventually found official expression in directives issued by the Allied Control Council, the highest power in Germany and the various zonal authorities. Among the most important was that on the reform of educational systems. This mammoth task was entrusted to my much admired friend Robert Birley, later headmaster of Eton, who was notably successful in carrying it out.

It was in furtherance of this policy of disclosing the German people to themselves that in June 1946 the British Foreign Office and the United States Department of State agreed jointly to publish documents from the archives of the German Foreign Ministry and the Chancellery, the object being 'to establish the record of German foreign policy preceding and during World War Two'. The two governments realised the unique nature of this enterprise and its magnitude and importance. Captured enemy documents had been published in the past, and the Germans had not hesitated to produce selections from the files of the governments of those countries they had overrun, chiefly Poland and France, but this had always been directed towards the support of some propaganda thesis. Now two victorious powers were setting out to establish the full record of the diplomacy of a vanquished power from captured archives 'on the basis of the highest scholarly objectivity'.

Each government was to nominate an editor-in-chief who should appoint his own staff, and who was not only permitted but enjoined to conduct his selection and editing with absolute freedom from governmental influence or interference. The responsibility for the resulting volumes was entirely theirs.

By a further provision of the Anglo-American agreement the two governments regarded themselves as 'free to publish separately any portion of the documents'. This was to prevent the exercise of veto by either editor upon the other and also to avoid a possible deadlock. To the best of my knowledge it was only exercised on one occasion, though under circumstances which, as will be seen, were mildly embarrassing.

I had known of the negotiations prior to this agreement and had even been slightly involved in a consultative capacity, but I had no idea that I should have any closer association with the project. However, I had not long returned from Nuremberg when I received a telephone call from my old friend Jim Passant, who had been a co-frequenter with me of The Taverne Group (as I have described in *Knaves, Fools and Heroes*) and had become the librarian and director of research at the Foreign Office. He was now inviting me on behalf of the Foreign Secretary to assume the position of British editor-in-chief of the captured German archives.

Deeply interested though I was, and not a little flattered at being selected to lead the British team in this unique project, I did not jump at it at once. I was desperately anxious to get my *Munich* finished and I had just taken on another job which threatened to be fairly time-consuming.

The University of Oxford had opened its arms widely in

68

welcome to returning warriors and many colleges had been at great pains to provide additional accommodation for their young men. As demobilisation progressed, however, it became apparent that, though the rising tide of new applicants might be contained physically, there were not enough professional dons and tutors to cope with their intellectual demands. An appeal went out for volunteers who would supplement the ranks and in pursuance of this Isaiah Berlin arrived at Garsington one afternoon to solicit my help. He knew that I had had some slight (*very* slight) teaching experience at the University of Virginia before the war and he now put it to me as my national duty to join New College as a temporary lecturer and tutor. I have never been able to refuse any request made by Isaiah and I thus found myself pledged to teach a course in P.P.E. (politics, philosophy and economics) for a period of five years. It proved to be a most entertaining experience and brought me a number of new friends, notably Alan Bullock, David Cecil and James Joll. It also caused the University to take executive action on making the horrifying discovery that I had no degree. They conferred on me an M.A. 'by decree', thus making me, as it were, respectable – or, at any rate, legitimate.

My pupils were of the greatest interest, ranging from my first tutorial, where I found myself dauntingly confronted by five ex-brigadiers averaging about twenty-six years in age, to Anthony Wedgwood Benn, who was not then what he is now!

I explained my predicament to Jim Passant and he promised to relay it to the Foreign Secretary; however my hand was forced by a personal letter from Ernie Bevin making a very strong case for my taking the job. I therefore made as graceful an acceptance as I could. I said that I *must* have time to finish my book (for which my publishers were champing), but that thereafter I would become editor-in-chief for a period of two years. In the view of the Foreign Office the whole project would be finished by then, and they were wholly incredulous when I assured them that we should be lucky if we got properly organised and succeeded in publishing two or three volumes in that space of time. Thirty years later the project is still incomplete, though the work is now carried on with German co-operation.

I duly finished *Munich*, which was published in 1948. It was, I believe, the first book to appear which made use of the vast amount of evidence made available by the Nuremberg Trials. Since its publication some thirty years ago much new material has come into the public domain in the relevant documents of the British Foreign Office and of the German Foreign Ministry and in a host of memoirs, contributing invaluably to the narrative of Munich by filling in details, but this does not alter in any way my general contention. This was as follows:

Let us say of the Munich Agreement that it was inescapable; that, faced with the lack of preparedness in Britain's armaments and defences, with the lack of unity at home and in the Commonwealth, with the collapse of French morale and with the uncertainty of Russia's capacity to fight, Mr Chamberlain had no alternative to do other than he did; let us pay tribute to his persistence in carrying out a policy which he honestly believed to be right. Let us accept and admit all these things, but in so doing let us not omit the shame and the humiliation which were ours; let us not forget that, in order to save our skins – that because we were too weak to protect ourselves – we were forced to sacrifice a small power to slavery. It is of no avail to say that we saved Czechoslovakia from that fate which was later suffered by our ally Poland; that, but for Munich, Bohemia and Moravia would have been devastated as were the provinces of Cracow and Lodz and Warsaw. In reality it was the Czechs who saved us; for, had President Beneš elected to fight with Russian support and thus precipitate an Eastern European War, it is impossible to believe that Britain and France could have kept aloof, however reluctantly they might have been dragged into participation.

I still believe this represents a true assessment of what happened at Munich.

Having completed this task I divided my time between New College and the Foreign Office. I chose a staff with some care, making a special effort to obtain the services of some of our assistants from the prosecution team at Nuremberg who had been familiar with the documentary material we were now handling in bulk. I also opened a correspondence with my American opposite number, Raymond Sontag, whom I had known when he was a star performer in the history department at Princeton and who had recently become head of the history department at the University of California at Berkeley. It was, indeed, to his seminar at Princeton that I had been talking when we received the news of the German breakthrough on 19 May 1940.

Ray was a fine historian and scholar, but he was somewhat overawed by his responsibilities as American editor-in-chief and his relations with the State Department were, I felt, more subservient than were mine with the Foreign Office.

I should add that in April 1947 the French Government adhered to the Publication Agreement, which meant that there was added to us Maurice Beaumont, a far greater historian and scholar than Sontag or myself, a man of delightful personality and authority. I have rarely admired more any man's intellectual capacity, which was of the highest French standard – no mean tribute in itself. Of all the starters in this peculiar project he is the only one who is still in there running!

At the outset, however, Ray and I were on our own and he very civilly flew over to confer with me on our immediate problems. The first of these was accommodation. The congestion at Marburg had become so great that a new home had to be found for both documents and editorial staff. It was appropriate that our operational base should be in Berlin and through the good offices of the Allied Control Council for Germany we were lucky enough to find space in the former premises of the old Radio Berlin, whence, ironically enough, Goebbels had for so long alternately perverted and exhorted the minds of the German people.

Our second problem was translation. It was, of course, our intention to publish our selected documents in German, but we reluctantly agreed that in both our countries there were too many people engaged in the study of German history whose knowledge of the language was insufficiently great to permit them to make full use of our volumes in the original. It was therefore decided that a parallel edition should be published in an English translation and we agreed on the method and procedure which should govern this work.

Thus was launched the great project of publishing the captured German archives, a labour of Hercules in itself with sometimes the frustration of Sisyphus.

What particularly pleased me about this new assignment was that it gave me a valid reason to renew my connections with Germany. I had paid one visit to Berlin soon after the conclusion of the Nuremberg Trials in order to inspect the Spandau jail together with its new occupants. This was also to fulfil my private pledge to myself, after my providential escape from the Night of the Long Knives, that I would never return to Germany until I could do so with the authority of a representative (however lowly) of a conquering and occupying power. I had been convinced in June 1934 that war with Germany had become inevitable sooner or later and it had not occurred to me that we should lose it. However, it had been twelve years before I could redeem my pledge.

Now, however, with old friends such as Pat Dean at the

head of the German Department of the Foreign Office and Sir William Strang and Christopher Steel as successive chief political advisers to the British element in Berlin, I was very strongly placed. After all, what is the good of being a victorious power if you don't take advantage of it? So I visited Berlin whenever possible.

These were the days when it was still our policy to make the Germans realise that they had lost the war, and the chief officials of the Allied occupation lived in style. The suburbs of the city had not suffered so greatly from bombing as the metropolis itself and it was possible to find perfectly adequate quarters. William and Elsie Strang lived in an enormous villa in the Grünewald, whose size earned it the nickname of 'The Palace'. It had been built by a rich Jewish banker in the early part of the century, then confiscated by some opulent Nazi boss and finally sequestrated as the official residence of the chief British political adviser. It was hideous, since neither of its previous owners seemed to have had any decorative taste at all, but comfortable in a sort of Teutonic-Edwardian way. Its rooms were capacious and its plumbing excellent if ostentatious. It was the general effect which was so remarkably ill-favoured. It was magnificently staffed by a detachment of Royal Marines, than whom there are no more efficient and considerate attendants, and cars with army drivers abounded. It was all very impressive.

When Kit Steel, later to be British Ambassador in Bonn, succeeded the Strangs, the first fine careless rapture of the Occupation had subsided and the establishment had been correspondingly diminished. The Palace had been abandoned and Kit and Kate lived in an extremely comfortable (and much nicer) house, also taken over from some Nazi hierarch. It was opposite the Palace and had a charming garden which sloped down to a small lake.

The Germans liked Kit Steel, partly because he took the trouble to understand them, and partly because with his high colouring and slightly choleric semi-military bearing he was the sort of Englishman whom they could understand.

Since Germany was still under a military occupation, Steel, although himself a civilian, had a few officers to supplement the regular career diplomats and one of them, a dashing figure in the khaki tunic and maroon trousers of the 'Cherry Pickers' (the 11th Hussars), was detailed to look after me on occasion. He proved to be an exceedingly entertaining companion named Alan Maclean, who after a brief subsequent diplomatic career has become a power in the publishing house of Macmillan and a devoted friend of Ruth and myself.

Another friendship founded in Berlin at this time had a double nature. The head of the American Military Intelligence was a Colonel Peter Rodes, who had three beautiful daughters who cut a swathe through the ranks of the occupation personnel, both military and civilian, British and American. The Colonel, who was rather a fierce man until you got to know him, and I had a good deal of interests in common, and Mrs Rodes was – and remains – a darling. I was always delighted to be asked to their house, and when I left for good at the time of the air lift I was truly sorry to say goodbye.

At this point there should be a row of asterisks. Some years later, however, I was invited by the University of Oxford to supervise the Ph.D. dissertation of a Rhodes Scholar from Princeton named James Hester, who had selected for his subject an obscure but important aspect of German-American relations after the First World War. Jim used to make the weary uphill journey from Pembroke College to Garsington once a week by bicycle, a feat which I admired as much for its physical achievement as for its academic devotion. We would discuss his current problems and then we would have lunch and continue our talks on more general topics.

Ruth and I both liked Jim Hester from the first. He was bright and cheerful and good-looking, and had a refreshingly keen mind which was never satisfied with any glib or incomplete answer. He might have made a great lawyer for he was quick to seize on any frailty of argument and made it apparent, with the greatest courtesy, that perhaps there was more to a statement that I had made – or perhaps less! I was very sure, even in those early days, that James Hester was marked by destiny for advancement and success, and he began in exactly the right way. To our delight he at length confided to us that he was engaged to Janet ('Jannie'), one of those beautiful Rodes daughters whom I had known in Berlin. Though he had known much success in his comparatively short life, Jim Hester never did a smarter thing, for Jannie is a superb person.

Within a surprisingly short space of time Jim had become, while still in his thirties, President of New York University, the largest private educational institution in the United States; he was the youngest university president in America. It was a *tour de force* and I was intensely proud of the young man who had become so much a part of our lives at Garsington and whose family we now regard as part of our own.

Later our careers crossed again. In 1967 he offered me the position of Visiting Professor of History in his university for the autumn term, an appointment which I held until 1970, when I could no longer withstand the rigours of New York's winter climate and was forced to retire. This however was not the end of my association with the university. In 1973 it was my heartfelt pleasure to receive an honorary degree of Doctor of Letters at the hands of my former pupil, Jim Hester.

To return to Berlin. No one who did not see the city in the years immediately following the end of the war can imagine the degree of devastation which prevailed. When I first went there in the winter of 1946 the streets were still filled with rubble, through which a way had been cleared for vehicles, and, though there had been a day when I thought

I knew the government quarter of the city *comme ma poche*, I found it simply impossible to direct my driver to the various landmarks which had once been so familiar. Moreover I noticed that even then, nearly eighteen months after the conclusion of hostilities, one still saw on the faces of the men and women in the streets that look of dazed bewilderment which one had encountered in London immediately after an air raid. They were still punch-drunk and weaving.

I remember my army driver taking me through the British sector, along the Charlottenburg-Chaussée through the Tiergarten, whose trees were being felled to provide the shivering Berliners with fuel, and stopping at my request at the top of the Sieges Allee. This had been an avenue of statues of the Hohenzollern margraves, electors, kings and emperors, and one of the more hideous collections of statuary in Europe. For some reason of his own Hitler had had its direction changed so that it ran east and west instead of north and south, and by a freak of fortune all its monstrosities had escaped virtually unharmed from the bombing. However, the rose garden at the far end had been trampled out of recognition. It had been the creation of Wilhelm II's first wife, the Empress Victoria-Augusta, and had been centred around a marble statue of Her Majesty, wearing an Edwardian garden-party costume, complete with picture-hat and veil. This had mercifully been considered expendable by Fate.

We drove into the Russian sector past the ruins of the Reichstag Palace, which I had once seen in flames, and on up Unter den Linden to the ruins of the Imperial Schloss, the palladium of Hohenzollern glory. I walked over some of the rubble and picked up two Iron Crosses with 'WII' on them dating from the First World War. Incidentally, the Russians have now levelled off and totally obliterated all vestiges of the former Imperial Palace.

Then back and along the Wilhelmstrasse to the great new Reichskanzlei, which Albert Speer had built for Hitler, and, most exciting of all, the famous bunker. The 'stately pleasure-dome' which the Führer had decreed was in a battered condition, but not sufficiently so to conceal its grossness and profound absence of taste. It had all the appearance and dimensions of a very bad Hollywood set of the 1930s, and I was delighted to find that the gigantic table, which had been generally believed to be marble, was in fact made of synthetic stone. I picked up a chunk of it as a souvenir, and later had it made into an ink-stand to give to Alan Bullock when he had written his great study of Hitler.

The bunker itself had apparently changed very little from the sordid scene so vividly depicted by Hugh Trevor-Roper in his *Last Days of Hitler*. The gloom and dirt and squalor were undisturbed; the blankets in the dog's sleeping compartment remained and smelt accordingly. The rooms were still littered with papers and other debris and in the grounds was the burned and seared site of the final funeral pyre. It may have been imagination, but the reek of death still seemed to pervade the whole place.

During this and subsequent visits I was allowed to attend sessions of the Allied Control Council, that supreme body in which the four great powers had vested the sovereignty of Germany. I recall my surprise when I first entered the handsome chamber in which they met, for it seemed familiar. At first I could not account for this, for I was pretty certain I had never been in the room before; and then it suddenly came to me. From photographs and films which I had seen I realised that this was none other than the hall in which the dreaded People's Court had held its sessions and where the harsh voice of Roland Freisler had browbeaten and humiliated countless victims of Nazi tyranny before condemning them to death. It was some consolation to think that he himself had met death in this room when a bomb had ended his infamous career. It was a neat historical irony that the destinies of Germany were now being disposed in the hall where justice had been held in mockery.

The arrangement of the place had, of course, been changed.

Now a great circular table dominated the scene and around it sat the four allied military governors. I sat with the British delegation behind the broad back of General Sir Brian Robertson (son of the famous First World War Field-Marshal 'Wullie' Robertson) and the narrower shoulders of his deputy, Major-General Nevile Brownjohn. Brian Robertson was a great man in many ways and ideal for this particular job, for his military career had embraced both combat and administrative experience. He was utterly impassive and patient, and he never missed a trick. Nevile Brownjohn ('B.J.') was a perfect foil for his chief. In addition to his many other admirable capacities, he had a fluent knowledge of Russian and was thus able to keep Brian informed of the asides and comments exchanged between his Soviet colleagues. He did this by means of notes, never giving himself away, and it was not until his final appearance at the Council before promotion to another post that he allowed himself the pleasure of saying farewell to his Soviet opposite numbers in effortless Russian – to their acute alarm and despondency.

B.J. was not only a wise colleague but also a good friend. We were both Malvernians and when years later I became chairman of the school's Council of Management I leaned heavily upon his sage counsel and I never found it to fail.

The other members of the Allied Control Council were a curiously assorted lot. The Frenchman, General Pierre Joseph Koenig, took a detached point of view, being both cynically and humorously impressed by the mutual antagonism existing between his American and Russian colleagues. General Lucius Clay, with his fierce aquiline features and piercing eyes, was the embodiment of American opposition to all things Soviet and General Vasili Sokolovsky gave as lively a performance of Soviet antagonism to American policies. There was between these two a mutual antipathy which one could sense and almost see. It was as though actual currents passed between them, creating an atmosphere of naked hostility. The chill wind of the cold war blew through the council chamber more than once, and it was no surprise when matters reached breaking point in the climatic episode of the Berlin airlift.

There was one occasion, however, on which General Sokolovsky did me a kindness. The chairmanship of the Council rotated monthly and it was customary for the outgoing chairman to give a party. Not unnaturally, there was some competition in this field. One particular visit of mine to Berlin coincided with the vacating of the chair by Sokolovsky and he gave a magnificent entertainment. There were lashings of vodka, a prodigality of caviar in blocks of ice representing swans and other objects, a superb display of *sekuska*, and quantities of the best Russian champagne, which is pleasantly dry. It was a great party and in the middle of it the General sent his A.D.C. across the room to summon me to his side. He had a square saturnine face which rarely smiled, but that evening he was putting his best foot forward. Through an interpreter he informed me that during the war the Soviet General Staff had translated my book on the Brest-Litovsk treaty (*The Forgotten Peace*) and had had an edition printed on the Red Army Press for a limited circulation. 'A very limited one, I should imagine,' I replied, remembering some of the things I had written about Stalin. It was perhaps a tactless remark, and the General smiled a grim and rather terrifying smile. 'Oh we omitted the introduction,' he countered (my remarks on Stalin were in the introduction). 'But you won't get any royalties out of us,' he laughed, his good humour returning, 'we printed it for private purposes.' 'I think you might let me have a couple of copies,' I said, and he nodded and smiled again. Shortly thereafter he was as good as his word and two copies duly reached me. Though I cannot read them (any more than I can read the Japanese editions of *Hindenburg* and *Nemesis of Power*), they are nice to have.

Ever since the units of General Hodges's U.S. First Army had begun to accumulate collections of German official documents in April 1945 rumours circulated in London and elsewhere about a mysterious dossier known only as the 'Marburg File'. At first its existence was merely hinted at, then its alleged contents was vehemently denied, but finally, as I became more closely associated with this new documentary world, I discovered that not only did the Marburg File exist but that its contents consisted of no less sensitive a subject than the relations which had existed between the Nazis and the Duke of Windsor in Madrid and in Lisbon during the summer of 1940.

This, however, was only the beginning of the Marburg File mystery. Neither my American co-editor nor I had ever seen it, and when we enquired about it we were officially informed that it had been abstracted from the collection at Schloss Marburg on the direct orders of the Supreme Commander himself. It was therefore by this time in the files of the rear echelon of SHAEF, which remained at Bushey, or less probably at its forward headquarters at Frankfurt.

Ray Sontag and I were agreed that our position as independent editors 'of the highest scholarly objectivity' would be rendered ludicrous if we allowed any documents whatsoever to be withheld from us without making the strongest possible protest – including the tendering of our resignations. Our use of such material, along with that of all the material contained in the German Foreign Ministry files, must be left to our joint discretion, and I myself was particularly anxious not to give my American colleague an excuse or an opportunity for implementing the 'escape clause' of the Anglo-American agreement which left each Government 'free to publish separately any portion of the documents'.

Having reached this decision, Ray Sontag returned to the United States, saying blandly that he was perfectly ready to leave its implementation in my hands, but would I please let him know in advance if I proposed to resign as he would have to make arrangements with his university to return to full-time employment.

It did not take me long to decide on my first step. I went unerringly to Moley Sargent at the Foreign Office. He, of course, knew of the existence of the Marburg File but had never seen it and he was horrified at its disappearance. 'We must go to the Secretary of State on this one,' he said, and there and then he took me upstairs to Mr Bevin's room. Ernie Bevin listened to our story in silence and then ruminated. 'This,' he said at last, 'is a 'ot potato. We've got to get the file back, and you,' he added to me, 'must 'ave a look at it and decide with your American friend what to do with it. But,' turning to Moley, 'I think we'll 'ave to tell the Palace.' So on the following day Moley took me along to Buckingham Palace to meet for the first time – but by no means the last – the King's Principal Private Secretary, Sir Alan Lascelles.

Of Tommy Lascelles I shall write in another chapter in a different connection, suffice it to say here that he was entirely co-operative. He and Moley were old friends and colleagues and were even somewhat alike in character and in their air of Edwardian elegance. The fact that I was a friend of Moley's counted considerably in my favour with Tommy and was to be helpful in our future relations – of which both of us were at this time in ignorance. He thanked us for informing him and said that he was sure that the King would share Mr Bevin's view. We then departed.

Much later I learned that the King already knew of the contents of the Marburg File, though it was not he who had requested its abstraction. Though I consider it highly improbable that General Eisenhower acted on his own initiative, I never knew (nor do I know to this day) whose initiative it was. The important consequence of the curious incident was that the Marburg File was speedily returned to our custody and that we duly included the bulk of its contents in the *Series D*, Vol. X, of those fat green volumes which were issued in due course by His Majesty's Stationery Office. Frances Donaldson has made good use of them in her admirable biography of King Edward VIII.

Another fascinating discovery among the archives was the Nazi black list compiled by the Gestapo and comprising the names of those who were to be arrested and consigned to concentration camps in the event of a successful invasion of Britain. I was gratified to find that I had won an 'honourable mention', along with many of my friends. Even more entertaining was the contents of the white list, in which were entered the roll of those who were regarded by the Gestapo as potential collaborators.

The firm foundation of bipartite solidarity and personal friendship on which the relations between Ray Sontag and me were based – and which was later broadened to include Maurice Beaumont – continued to inspire our co-operation throughout the time we worked together. I can recall no occasion on which we disagreed fundamentally in our difficult task of selection. Although we might not, at first glance, attach the same degree of importance to some specific document, an amicable discussion would convince one of us of the superior wisdom of the other's judgement.

When it is remembered that we were rendering down between three and four hundred tons of documents into a form suitable for publication by means of informed and adequate selection, the magnitude of our task may begin to be appreciated. There were all sorts of difficulties, both technical and human, to be overcome. We learned only by trial and error the limitation of the available material and the problems inherent in exploiting and developing disordered and incomplete files. We eventually had at our disposal more than a million pages of microfilms covering the most important documents from 1914 to 1945. Since, however, our initial object was to deal with Nazi foreign policy we began our researches at January 1933.

At the outset the selection of documents was made from the microfilm version by historians working in London, Washington and Paris. This method proved, however, to be too cumbersome, and it was agreed that the preliminary selection should be made by an international team of British, American and French historians working on the original files, leaving the final selection to the periodic conferences of the editors-in-chief.

Since our objective was to present to the world an understanding of German foreign policy, we soon discovered that this could not be gained from a study of inter-office documentation only. The German estimates of the policy of other powers was one of the most important factors shaping German policy, and these therefore had also to be weighed and included. We realised, of course, that these reports from abroad were full of pitfalls for the unwary. German diplomats in foreign countries all too often reported in style and matter what they thought would please Hitler, and even those who felt compelled to convey unpleasant tidings did so in language calculated to carry conviction to the Nazi party leaders.

The German diplomatic service both at home and abroad was deeply divided. Some embraced, at least for a time, the tenets of the Nazi faith; some were sincerely opposed to much of what came their way but remained in the service, as they explained, 'to keep a worse man out'; some were merely concerned for their pensions. For his part the Führer kept most of them in his employ only because he found them indispensable. He realised that there were few amongst his followers who would commend themselves to the foreign ministries and chancelleries of the world, and he therefore retained the professionals. But he did not trust them – sometimes with reason – and more often than not he kept them in ignorance of his own innermost planning. The archives of the German Foreign Ministry suffered accordingly.

These then were some of the lions in our path, and the fact that we were able to produce anything at all, and especially as a result of general agreement, was in itself something of a tribute to the character of our international historical scholarship.

It will be remembered that the Anglo-American agreement, under which we operated, contained an 'escape clause' whereby each Government reserved the right to publish separately any portion of the documents. In so far as I had given any grave consideration to this matter I had imagined that a situation would arise in which Raymond Sontag and I, and later Maurice Beaumont, after an amicable discussion, would 'agree to disagree' and that one or other of us would say, 'O.K., chaps, I shall recommend my government to publish these documents independently,' and that would be that. What I had certainly never envisaged was that the escape clause would be used as a secret weapon, yet this is exactly what occurred.

We had reached an editorial decision to begin our publication with the Austrian *Anschluss* of 1938 and proceed thence chronologically. Our work of selection, however, far outran the process of production, and in the course of it we had come across a remarkable collection of documents giving the inside story, from the German point of view, of the negotiations preceding and following the signature of the Nazi-Soviet pact in August 1939. These we agreed to publish in due course and in their historical order, though I remember saying to Ray that it was a pity we couldn't get them out earlier, because at Nuremberg the emphasis had been laid on the Nazi aggression against the Soviet Union in 1941 rather than on their earlier collaboration in crime.

Those proved to be prophetic words. By the winter of 1947 the cold war was very much in evidence, and the State Department conceived the bright idea of using these documents to embarrass the Russians and to expose their villainy. Ray Sontag, ever an ardent cold warrior, and his assistant, James Beddie, were instructed to skim the cream from the dossier in question and compress it into a short volume which would be made public under the imprimatur of the Department of State. This work was carried on in great seclusion, and so great was the degree of secrecy imposed upon them that no whisper of their activities reached London at any level, neither governmental nor editorial, until the completed work burst upon the world with a blaze of publicity early in 1948. In an unsigned preface the fact that the escape clause existed was mentioned, together with the announcement that 'the Department of State has decided to publish separately the most significant documents bearing on German-Soviet relations during 1939–1941.'

I was not wholly pleased. To begin with I considered it a breach of our editorial co-operation that I should not have been informed in advance. I was certainly as warm a supporter of the cold war as Ray Sontag and, had I been consulted, I would certainly have agreed to the speeding-up of publication as a joint effort. Secondly, I felt that, though technically legal, the action of the United States government constituted a breach, if not of the letter most certainly of the spirit, of the escape clause. The secrecy of their operation implied a lack of confidence in both the Foreign Office and in me, and also some measure of disagreement between Ray Sontag and myself as to whether the documents should be published. Nothing could have been further from the truth.

Ray, when we met at our next editorial conference, was both shamefaced and apologetic, and I readily acquit him of any personal responsibility for this unfortunate affair. It was, I fear, his profound veneration for the State Department which compelled his acquiescence in their conduct. I am happy to say that this rupture in our usually friendly relations did not last long and that we subsequently published the entire collection.

The year 1948, which had begun thus inauspiciously, was to prove of considerable importance to the world, to the German documents project and to myself in connection with it. The icy wind of the cold war, the early breezes of which I had observed in the sessions of the Allied Control Council in Berlin, was now in full blast and rapidly approaching hurricane force. The Russian rejection of the Marshall Aid plan in July 1947 had, in effect, drawn the battle lines, and a year later the cold war was in full swing. That outer bastion of Western democracy, Czechoslovakia, had fallen in February 1948, to be followed by the signing of the Brussels Pact on 17 March between Britain, France and the Benelux countries for their mutual defence against aggression, and the genesis of NATO.

In Germany the two divisions were drawing rapidly apart. The Soviet Union tightened its grip on its own zone and its adjoining sector of Berlin, while the British, American and French governments had unified their zones economically and politically and were headed towards the establishment of a Western German Republic. These activities in their turn provoked lively protests from the Russians, who denounced the western powers for wrecking the inter-Allied control of Germany.

In Berlin itself the climate of thought was tense with crisis. On 20 March General Sokolovsky accused his western colleagues of 'tearing up the agreement on control machinery' and 'destroying the Control Council and burying it'. He then stalked out of the Council chamber. This, for practical purposes, may be said to mark the close of inter-Allied control of Germany, as laid down in the agreement signed in May 1945.

The flashpoint of explosion was now imminent. On both sides hostility increased and the only question remaining in the minds of many was what particular upshot would provide the break. It happened to be a fiduciary issue. On 18 June, the three western powers introduced a reformed Deutschmark into their three zones to meet the inflationary situation. The Russian riposte was immediate and apparently decisive. Apart from issuing their own reformed currency – which they proposed to introduce into the whole of Berlin as well as the Soviet zone – they imposed a blockade on the western sectors of the city. On 24 June all land and water traffic was halted indefinitely on 'technical' grounds.

The western allies met this challenge with courage and initiative. There followed the Berlin airlift, perhaps the most dramatic confrontation of the cold war, and certainly one of the most remarkable technical achievements of modern aviation. For 323 days British and American aircraft landed, at five-minute intervals, sufficient supplies to maintain life in West Berlin at a reasonable level. Starting with an irreducible minimum they persistently raised their level of cargoes even in bad weather. The tonnage of imported supplies climbed steadily until in the spring of 1949 the average figure was 8000 tons a day. There could not have been a more comprehensive proof that the Soviet blockade had failed and that the Kremlin had sustained a major diplomatic defeat.

It was as a result of this sequence of events and its dramatic climax that some vitally important decisions were called for on the part of the editors-in-chief of the documentary project. Though a great deal of our material had been microfilmed and copies existed in London, Paris and Washington, the precious originals, on which the initial research and selection were based, were still housed in the Telefunken Building in the American sector of Berlin. It can be imagined what a rich prize this would have proved for the Russians should it fall into Soviet hands, especially since the publication of the German documents on the Soviet-Nazi Pact. What then should be done about them?

When the great airlift operation was originally launched there was no certainty what, if any, measures of retaliation the Soviet authorities in Berlin would take. Would they, for example, try to prevent the British and American aircraft from landing? Would they indulge in reprisals against individual Germans? Finally, would they go all the way and employ force in an attempt to occupy the sectors held by the western powers? Were we, in fact, within measurable distance of the outbreak of the Third World War, for there was no doubt that force would be met with force?

In so far as the British were concerned the situation was somewhat complicated by the fact that the period for which I had contracted to be editor-in-chief was drawing to its close and the Foreign Office had, at my suggestion, begun a search for my successor, so that he might work with me for the last few months thereby learning the tricks of the trade before taking over. It had not occurred to me that it would be a difficult job to find someone who would be willing and qualified to take on the job, but, as not infrequently happens in such circumstances, the authorities decided to appoint two persons to do the work which I had done alone. They eventually came up with a suggestion which, on the face of it, did not seem too happy a combination. They appointed as joint British editors-in-chief James Joll and General James Marshall-Cornwall.

James Joll was already a friend of mine and a colleague at New College, and we were both destined to be founding Fellows of St Antony's College, of which James became Sub-Warden. He is, in my opinion, among the best of our modern historians teaching and writing today, with a clear sweep of historical perspective and persuasive judgement in the fields of the mid-nineteenth and twentieth centuries.

James Marshall-Cornwall had once been the youngest full General in the British Army and has in later years become the author of excellent military biographies. He had been military attaché in Berlin in the closing years of the Weimar Republic and had seen the rise of the Nazi movement at first hand.

At first sight it might seem that they constituted a curiously assorted team. James Joll is politically to the left of the Liberal party, while the General is decidedly right of centre. In effect, however, they proved to be admirably complementary. James Joll had the scholarly historical expertise and James Marshall-Cornwall the practical military experience, and both were fluent in German. Between them they provided a first-class editorial combination, and the volumes of documents which appeared under their direction may truly be described as being 'of the highest scholarly objectivity'.

It was we three, therefore, who were faced with making the decisions on the British side for the future of the documents. We consulted our American and French colleagues and the Foreign Office communed with the State Department and with Berlin. Pat Dean was a tower of strength, taking time from what were, after all, more important aspects of the crisis to give me the benefit of his wise counsel.

At length we were all agreed. Since it did not seem likely that the Russians were about to take any violent means to prevent the continued operation of the airlift, the immediate danger of the American sector being overrun and the documents falling into Soviet hands might be discounted. However, it was decided as being highly desirable to remove them to a safer home, namely to England, and to continue our work there.

A full-dress conference, at which the new British editors-in-chief designate were to meet their American and French opposite numbers, had been laid on to meet in Berlin early in July and it would now have the additional responsibility of arranging for the evacuation of our documentary holdings, partly by air in returning aircraft, and partly by sea from Hamburg.

Thus it was that I flew to Berlin for the last time on 4 July 1948. It had been something of an effort to persuade the Americans to sacrifice the celebration of their national holiday, but in deference to the exigencies of the circumstances they had done so and acquired merit thereby. The conference went off well and smoothly. I was in the chair because it was the last time that I should attend one of these meetings as leader of the British group. At my suggestion it was agreed that my two successors should take over from me as soon as the re-establishment and reorganisation of the documents in England had been completed, and they in their turn asked me to remain as historical adviser to the project. I was very glad to do so and I held this post until 1956.

We finished our business on 6 July and were to fly home on the following day. I made my farewells to Raymond Sontag and Maurice Beaumont and we exchanged the usual compliments, then I borrowed a car and driver from Kit Steel, with whom I was staying, and set out to say good-bye to Berlin, for my dæmon was very insistent that this would be my last visit there. I had known the place well in good times and bad. I had seen it in the bourgeois frenetic days of the Weimar Republic, in the first hysteria of the Third Reich and later during the Brown Terror, and later still as a dazed and defeated city. Yet though we had been on familiar terms I had never liked Berlin. It had never charmed me as have Paris and New York. It was always interesting but it lacked enchantment.

Now, however, I felt a definite admiration for the toughness of these citizens of the beleaguered city. They were calm in the face of impending danger and confident in the ability of the British and the Americans to sustain and protect them. Headed by their splendid Oberburgermeister, Ernst Reuter, a veteran of the Weimar Social Democrats, they displayed a remarkable courage and endurance which one could not but respect. One felt proud of them as a bulwark of democracy, and for the first and only time I experienced that feeling of shared comradeship which President Kennedy expressed some years later in another and similar crisis: '*Ich bin ein Berliner.*'

THE BARE BONES OF HISTORY

It was a beautiful summer's day and the magnolias were in bloom. Much had been done to restore order and cleanliness since my last visit and I was impressed by this as I drove about the streets, going within a respectful distance of the Soviet sector. I finished my tour of farewell at the little park which surrounds the Hohenzollern mausoleum at Charlottenburg. Here all was trim and well kept, deserted except for two little girls who were having a dolls' tea-party on the steps of the building's classical façade. I greeted them and they smiled cheerfully. I asked if the place were open and they pointed to a padlock on the door. Then one of them said roguishly, 'But you can get in at the back. The door's broken down and we go in to see the big boxes sometimes.' I followed her directions and found that the back entrance had indeed been broken in. A bomb had damaged the system of pipes which presumably had ventilated the vault for these lay twisted and broken inside the entrance. I stepped over this obstacle and in the half-light which filtered in I found myself confronted by a coffin showing no signs of disrepair. I looked at the name plate and found that it was the casket of Queen Louisa of Prussia, that valiant consort of Frederick-William III, who had defied Napoleon. I did not go further but paid my silent respects. As I drove home I reflected on the curious circumstances which had ordained that my connection with the German Foreign Ministry Documents Project should begin and end with the coffin of a Hohenzollern.

This, however, was not quite my last contact with Berlin. In the February of the following year (1949) the Foreign Office decided that some measure of relief and recognition be accorded to Ernst Reuter for the constant watch and ward which he, as their Oberburgermeister, had kept over the citizens of West Berlin. They invited him to England for a brief holiday and Pat Dean asked me if Ruth and I would give him lunch at Garsington. We were delighted, of course. I remembered him as one of the few leading members of his party in the latter days of Weimar who had shown real statesmanship and understanding of the dangers of the Nazi menace, and his recent performance had been magnificent.

He came with Pat and a young friend of ours from the German Department named Peter Ramsbotham, both of whom were later destined to become Ambassadors at Washington. It was still difficult to provide a decent meal but Ruth put her best foot forward, which is always a very good foot indeed, and I went to some pains to procure some Bernkastler Riesling, which I knew would please any Berliner. Reuter was highly pleased. Whatever our food problems might be they were considerably less than those of his besieged city, and he also appreciated to the full the beauties of Garsington – even in winter. We had a good time gossiping about Weimar and our common friends in the politics of that period.

It was a cold day, though sunny, and there was still some snow on the ground, but after lunch we paced up and down the lawn, he in his famous blue beret cocked at an angle worthy of Cyrano de Bergerac himself above his grey locks and his keen sensitive face, and I remember feeling glad that we could do something to please this brave man. He was so grateful to the western powers for their support of his city, so ready to share in their defiance, so confident of their success. 'Had it not been for you we should have disappeared into the Soviet zone,' he said simply.

I remember thinking, too, that here was a man who in future years could provide a Chancellor for Germany and a leader for the Social Democratic Party. I believe I should have been justified in this belief had Reuter lived. He was a man of great culture, high principle and supreme integrity, having the statesmanship of an Adenauer and lacking the theatrical hysteria of a Schumacher and the well-meaning wishful thinking of a Willy Brandt. Alas, he died in September 1953.

CHAPTER FOUR

Nemesis of Power

Early in 1948 Archie Clark Kerr, Lord Inverchapel, retired
as ambassador to Washington, and the British government
decided to replace him by a non-career ambassador. Their
choice was Sir Oliver Franks who, like many of the leading
academic figures at Oxford where he had been Provost of
The Queen's College, had become a highly successful temporary civil servant during the war. At that time he became
Director of Labour at the Ministry of Supply and in this
capacity he came to know Ernest Bevin, then Minister of
Labour. Indeed, he not infrequently exercised a balsamic
influence on Bevin's bitter confrontations with Lord Beaver-
brook when the latter was the Minister of Production. It
was natural, therefore, that when, later in 1947, Ernie Bevin,
then Foreign Secretary, looked around for someone to make
the Marshall Aid plan work administratively, he wisely
turned to Oliver Franks, who again forsook The Queen's
College to tackle the far from easy task of setting up the
Organisation for European Economic Co-operation.

Oliver's appointment as ambassador to Washington was an
inspired choice, for he was exactly the type of person who
could share the wavelength of that great triumvirate
then directing American policies, President Truman, Dean
Acheson and General Marshall. Not only did he have some
personal experience of the United States, having served as
a Visiting Professor of Economics at the University of
Chicago before the war, but he instinctively possessed that
same understanding of the American scene and character
which I had known so well in Philip Lothian.

This was, in fact, why I came into this story at all. Oliver

Franks had expressed to the Foreign Office the desire for someone to accompany him to whom he could 'let down his hair' as one non-professional to another, and the Office, slightly smarting from having temporarily lost the Washington embassy for the Career, was equally anxious that this individual should be someone whom they at least knew and found acceptable. The upshot was an invitation to me from Moley Sargent in February to go to Washington with Oliver Franks, with the rank of Counsellor of Embassy.

The proposition had a tremendous attraction. Both Ruth and I love Washington, which was also a convenient distance from her home in Charlottesville, and she would, I knew, be a natural for diplomatic life. A house in Georgetown, where we already had many friends, would have been a delight. Though I did not then know Oliver Franks and his wife Barbara, I had a great admiration for all that I had heard of him and for his achievements and would have much liked to have served under him.

On the other hand, there were strong negative factors. I was pledged to New College for the remaining three of my five years and still held the post of editor-in-chief of the captured German Foreign Ministry Archives, though this was due to end at the close of the year. I did not want to acquire a reputation for taking up appointments and then dropping them unfinished in order to take on others. Moreover, I had already held the position offered on a very intimate basis of friendship with Philip Lothian, a basis which had given me a considerable independence of the Chancery. And on the purely personal side, I was most anxious to begin my new book *The Nemesis of Power*.

Ruth, at this moment, was on the high seas returning from her annual visit to her mother in Virginia. I was saddened by these yearly separations, though I fully understood the need for them. I also deeply regretted that I myself was cut off from America for the longest period ever. The fact, however, that the Treasury regulations prohibited the ordinary traveller from taking more than £25 out of the country during any one year precluded one from wandering far.

I consulted her discreetly by letter without disclosing details or names and we found we were of one mind. Like me, she was inimical to uprooting ourselves from a home which we had so lately established, and I knew that it would be particularly difficult for her since, as an American, she had, with infinite pains, successfully adjusted herself to strange surroundings and to feeling at home. Standing amid the alien corn she had just begun to reap a harvest.

Yet I was loath to let the Foreign Office down and I did not wish to appear discourteous to Oliver Franks, for whose record I had every admiration. I did not, in fact, want to refuse the offer, which after all was a very gratifying one, without proposing an alternative.

Then light dawned upon me, and I marvelled that I had not thought earlier of the solution. I have written in *Special Relationships* of Aubrey Morgan and his wife Constance, with whom I had been so closely associated as colleagues and friends in America during the early years of the war. Aubrey had ended the war as head of the British Information Services in New York amid universal acclaim, and had retired to farm on the borders of Washington and Oregon, where he had raised a splendid herd of dairy cattle.

Here, I thought, was a reasonable excuse to summon Cincinnatus from his plough – or at least from his milk pail. With his wide knowledge of the American scene he would be an invaluable adjunct to any ambassador and his extensive wartime experience had given him a powerful insight into the machinations and bewildering byways of the world of public relations. Aubrey was, in fact, infinitely better qualified and equipped for the role of confidant to Oliver Franks than I was, and so I represented him to Moley Sargent a month later.

Moley was not so easily convinced as I had hoped. 'I

seem to remember some difficulties with the Chancery,' he murmured. I persisted. 'You'll be exceedingly lucky if you get him at all. Let me see if I can persuade him to come over, without telling him why, and then bring Oliver Franks and him together. It couldn't possibly do any harm and I have an odd feeling that they would get on famously.' My dæmon had convinced me of this.

Moley was still somewhat dubious, but he let me have my way and I returned to Garsington to put through the longest distance telephone call I had ever made in my life, some six thousand miles. Since the whole affair was still cloaked in official secrecy I was not able to be very explicit. When I got Aubrey on the line I asked him, 'Can you trust me well enough to fly over here at once on what I may call a matter of national interest?' He was non-committal but promised to consider the idea and let me know.

I was mildly disappointed, but I had reckoned without the wily deviousness of Moley Sargent. On reflection he had become convinced by my earlier arguments and, without telling me, had authorised the embassy at Washington to sound out Aubrey as to his willingness to accept the offer. This duty was performed by D'Arcy Edmondson, a friend and former B.I.S. colleague of ours (he later became Consul-General in Boston) who was spending Easter with the Morgans in the state of Washington.

Moley was spending the Easter week-end (26–29 March) with me at Garsington, and in the midst of our post-prandial talk beside the wood fire on Sunday evening the telephone rang and the operator asked me to take a trans-atlantic call from Washington. I had been vaguely expecting a call from Raymond Sontag on some detail of editorial problems relevant to the German documents, and I invited Moley to listen in on another line. This was not, as it turned out, a very happy idea. It was Aubrey calling from the great north-west of America in something of a temper and with a fine disregard for security or secrecy.

He said he couldn't make out what the hell I or the Foreign Office wanted of him. He wanted to know why he should be appointed a Counsellor of Embassy when he had already been one and resigned from it. He wanted to know a lot of things that I would just as soon he had not asked with the Permanent Secretary to the Foreign Office listening in. Moley, of course, enjoyed it all hugely – especially my embarrassment. 'I thought you said Morgan was an easy person to deal with,' he said later. 'He sounds rather a fire-brand to me.'

I did my best to stem the tide of Aubrey's voluble acerbity and to repeat my request that he come to England and discuss the matter in detail – and perhaps more rationally. As D'Arcy Edmondson, *in situ*, gave him the same advice, Aubrey eventually capitulated and arrived in England on 17 April, coming straight to me at Garsington.

One of the most agreeable aspects of my friendship with Aubrey is that we can bridge a gap of years in ten minutes, and now sitting in the Oak Room at Garsington it was no time before we were gossiping away as if we were still colleagues in New York. At length I broached the main point. Aubrey still wanted more details. 'What sort of a chap is Franks?' he asked. 'I don't know,' I said, 'I've never seen him.' Aubrey seemed surprised. 'Do you mean to say you've brought me all this way to meet a man you don't know?' he asked. 'He doesn't know you either,' I replied, and I went on to give details of Oliver's career and his manifest suitability for the Washington appointment. 'All I'm asking you to do is to meet him,' I concluded. 'You may take a couple of instant dislikes, but I've a hunch you won't.'

I realised that there were certain risks involved in my optimism. They were a contrasting, if complementary, pair. Oliver is quiet, reserved and rarely speaks until he has mastered a subject and has some concrete offering to make.

97

D

Aubrey is ebullient and outgoing, a brilliant talker but also a willing and informed listener.

It happened, therefore, that a few days later on a fair April evening (22 April) Oliver and Aubrey and I dined with Isaiah Berlin at New College, and the two of them talked at length as they strolled up and down the famous gardens. Isaiah and I watched anxiously; the auguries seemed, we thought, to be favourable – as indeed they proved to be. In the meantime Ruth had returned and a few days later Oliver and Barbara lunched at Garsington with Aubrey and ourselves, and a second long colloquy occurred between the two principals, during which the matter was clinched.

From this partnership there developed a marriage of minds as fruitful in friendship as it was productive in the line of duty. Oliver Franks is the first to pay tribute to Aubrey's contribution to his outstanding success as an ambassador, and Aubrey, once he has given his loyalty, is unshakable.

When my sister and her husband let Garsington Manor during the war they moved into Oxford to a house in Woodstock Road, which, though not a thing of beauty in itself, was easy to run in wartime and conveniently near the shops and colleges. With wonderful kindness Irene and Trevor allowed Ruth and me to make this our headquarters during the weeks which separated our return to England from our settling into the manor in April of 1946, making daily trips out to Garsington to supervise developments.

My brother-in-law would sometimes bring home colleagues of his from Christ Church and among them I met a rising young historian named Hugh Trevor-Roper. Hugh had served in Intelligence during the war and at its close had been given by the Supreme Commander, General Eisenhower, one of the most fascinating assignments it is possible to imagine. It was of the greatest importance to establish beyond peradventure the fact that Hitler was dead and also, as nearly as possible, the circumstances of his death. This was partly to avoid the appearance of a 'false Demetrius' in the future and also to remove much of the danger which might accrue from the alleged 'Werewolf Movement' who were said to believe in the survival of the Führer. It was Hugh's task therefore to reconstruct, as soon as possible after the Allied occupation of Berlin, the sordid and squalid happenings in the Chancellery bunker during that last episode of the Third Reich, and also to establish whether that funeral pyre which had blazed in the Chancellery garden had really consumed the bodies of Adolf Hitler and his recently married wife, Eva Braun.

The result of Hugh's brilliant detective work, conducted with the meticulous care of a trained historian, was a report giving a vivid narrative of the preceding events and a conclusive judgement that Hitler and his consort of a few days had indeed been consumed in the flames. When I talked with him he was expanding this admirable document into a book, the bulk of which he allowed me to read. Macmillan ultimately published it under the title of *The Last Days of Hitler*, and it at once brought its author international fame and started him off on a distinguished career leading to the Regius Professorship of Modern History at Oxford.

I mention this episode not only as a tribute to Hugh Trevor-Roper, but because it influenced my own decision in formulating the original design and scope of my next book, *The Nemesis of Power*. I had long intended to write an account of the abortive plot on Hitler's life of 20 July 1944, as a result of which various friends and acquaintances had ended their lives by the hangman's noose or the executioner's bullet. It would, I thought, be a splendid idea to model the book on Hugh Trevor-Roper's book, a comparatively brief and succinct study of the conspiracy and its failure.

Laudable though this intention may have been and granting that imitation is the sincerest form of flattery, I was soon to find that my original plan was not suited to the treatment of my subject. Hugh's study was of an isolated period with a definite end in view, but, as I pursued my preliminary planning and my researches, I found that this was far from true in my case. The plot of 20 July was the tragic and futile culmination of a whole period of history, and in studying it I found that I had to explain so much to myself in the way of preliminary facts – yet facts essential to the understanding of the conclusion – that these happenings would have to be deployed and explained to any student of the period. I realised, therefore, that I must abandon the idea of a compact study of an isolated incident and resign myself to writing an account of the German army in politics, from its humiliating defeat in November 1918 to its even more deeply humiliating capitulation in May 1945, explaining the strong degree of support it had originally given Hitler and how this support had waned and dwindled until military figures had joined with political personalities in an elaborate if amateurish conspiracy to murder the Führer and overthrow the Nazi regime. In addition, there was the civilian element in the resistance movement which could by no means be ignored.

I had had first-hand experience of the Seekt and Schleicher periods of the *Reichswehr* and of its brief honeymoon with Hitler which began to wane with the Night of the Long Knives in June 1934. Many of my officer friends had been associated – most of them fatally – with the plot of July 1944. I had also been in contact with a number of the civilian conspirators: Goerdeler and Adam von Trott in the United States, Helmuth von Moltke in Oxford, the Kordt brothers, Theo and Erich, during their comings and goings between London and Berlin, and, above all, Dietrich Bonhoeffer, in the heart of whose family in Berlin the tiny flame may be said to have been kindled.

I understand that Dietrich's theological principles are controversial and subject to criticism. On this I am not qualified to judge. What I do know is that, when I used to

see him during his pastorate at the Lutheran Church in
London in the thirties, I was convinced that I was in the
company of a saint and a saint of the most practical and
modern pattern. He had the appearance of a roly-poly
student, a delicious sense of humour, an unswerving faith
in God and a dauntless courage. I shall never forget how in
1935, when he announced his intention of returning to
Germany to take part in the struggle of the Confessional
Church against the Nazis, some of us tried to dissuade him
on the grounds of personal danger. He put us aside with
that appreciation of our thought for him and yet that calm,
indomitable refusal of our request with which Christ responded to those who, at the close of his ministry, sought to
keep him from making his final progress to Jerusalem.

It was through these connections, and also a close study
of the multifarious literature – most of it exculpatory –
which was pouring out of Germany in the immediate post-
war years, that I came to understand something of the
hideous dilemma with which certain Germans were confronted in the conflict of their own consciences. It is one
thing to be a member of a resistance movement in a country
occupied by a brutal invader, whose activities it is one's
clear-cut duty to sabotage and defeat, but it is quite another
to participate in a conspiracy against one's own government
and country. There are few greater agonies in the world
than that of divided loyalty. Especially is this true for men
who decide to follow a course of conduct which may lead
to the destruction of their fatherland in order to assure the
preservation of its soul and its ultimate rehabilitation as a
member of world society.

The resolution of an individual or a group to resist tyranny
and oppression by their fellow countrymen presupposes a
searching appraisal of the meaning and interpretation
of the term 'patriotism', which the dictionary defines as
'love for, and loyalty to, one's country'. Those who banded
together in Germany against Hitler had at the very outset

to make clear to themselves how far their actions would
cut across their own traditional concepts of patriotism,
how far they would go in the evolution of a new concept,
and how far they were themselves prepared to be called
traitors in the course of so doing. Some arrived at this clarity
of thought at an early date, some at a much later period;
some never achieved it at all and only jumped on the band-
wagon of resistance at a moment when 'treason was no
crime' and might indeed serve to erase the stain which earlier
Nazi associations had placed upon their records.

I have tried to show in *Knaves, Fools and Heroes* the
substantial degree of support which Hitler received from the
German people when he came to power in 1933 and the
reasons for its magnitude. It was against this general con-
donation, this mass placability, that Dietrich Bonhoeffer
inveighed until the final moment of his execution in 1944.
To him at least it was clear that, though primarily the guilt
for the misery and death and destruction which had been
loosed on Germany and upon the world would lie with
Hitler and the Nazi regime, the German people as a whole,
because of their active connivance in – or, at best, their
passive acceptance of – National Socialism and the gains that
it had brought to Germany, must bear a heavy burden of
responsibility. National Socialism was evil and so, therefore,
were all its fruits. There must be no question of retaining
for Germany that which she had gained by such means.

Dietrich never faltered; he was ready to go on to the end
with the ruthless work which he regarded as having been
delegated to the conspirators by divine grace. 'Hitler is
anti-Christ,' he declared. 'Therefore we must go on with
our work, and eliminate him whether he be successful or
not.' But, he added, their action in removing Hitler must
not be prompted by motives of revenge, of expediency or
even of punishment, but of repentance. 'There must be
punishment by God. We should not be worthy of such a

solution. We do not wish to escape repentance. Our action must be considered as an act of repentance.'

There were – perhaps understandably – but few among Dietrich's fellow conspirators who adhered to his doctrine of exculpatory immolation. Devoted and courageous though many of them were, men and women of the greatest integrity and probity, they were either unable or unwilling to accept the deep and basic truth that, by responding to Hitler's blandishments and placing him in power, the German people as a whole had committed a crime, for which not only penitence but atonement was demanded. A strong bond between them was not only their bitter opposition to Nazi tyranny, but also a deep sense of patriotic nationalism. What they plotted to do was no mere attempt upon a wicked ruler, or even a tyrant, but an act of salvation for Germany, an attempt to save her from future disasters and, as a corollary, to save as much as possible of what she already held and, perhaps, a little bit more. Moreover, for many of the military figures who eventually became involved in the conspiracy the basis of opposition to Hitler and his policies was that they endangered the national security and inviability of the Reich rather than that they were *unsittlich* (immoral).

If I found it difficult in the course of my researches to analyse, for myself and for others, the complex motives and precepts of German resistance, no such problem presented itself in discovering the cause of the failure of the conspiracy. This was simple in the extreme. The conspirators lacked among them a dedicated assassin. This was in no case prompted by cowardice but by the genuine desire of many in the conspiracy to play some part in the rebuilding of the structure of the new Germany.

To be a successful tyrannicide requires a complete single-ness of purpose, a recognition that the action meditated and planned is an end in itself. It demands a dedication which transcends the love of life and takes as a foregone conclusion the virtual certainty of death. It needs courage and self-sacrifice of a very special nature.

If, for example, on that fatal summer morning in East Prussia, 20 July 1944, Claus von Stauffenberg had been content to devote himself to the success of his primary project – the killing of Hitler – he would have remained in the conference room at Rastenburg and thus prevented my old riding companion, the well-meaning but inept Colonel Heinz Brandt, from moving the briefcase containing the bomb from where von Stauffenberg had left it within a few feet of the Führer to the other side of the baulk of timber supporting the table, thus protecting Hitler from the full blast of the explosion.

Count von Stauffenberg might indeed have lost his own life but he would have achieved his object. However, though a courageous man, he was not of the stuff of which dedicated assassins are made. He greatly desired to be one of the leading architects of the new Germany and was already destined for the post of State Secretary for War in Karl Goerdeler's provisional government. Indeed it was believed by many that, though free from all taint of personal or self-seeking pride, he might well have dominated by sheer force of personality both General Ludwig Beck, the prospective Regent, and Karl Goerdeler, the Chancellor-designate. As it was, he was shot that same evening in the courtyard of the Bendlerstrasse when the plot had failed.

To the best of my belief there were but two among the conspirators who fulfilled completely the qualifications of a dedicated assassin – and they were frustrated.

The first was Colonel Freiherr Rudolf von Gersdorf, who, on 21 March 1943, at the *Heldengedenktag* ceremonies at the Zeughaus on Unter den Linden, volunteered to stand close to Hitler and assassinate him at the risk of his own life. As he described the event to me in Bonn some ten years later, von Gersdorf said that he carried two bombs in the pockets of his tunic, each set with a delayed-action fuse set to explode in twenty minutes. This would, presumably, have killed both of them, but the Führer left after eight minutes, leaving his would-be assassin with the delicate task of de-activating his bombs. Von Gersdorf not only survived the war but also, even more miraculously, the avenging wrath of Himmler. He eventually became director of the West German national stud. A few years ago he sustained severe injuries to his spine as a result of a riding accident, which has condemned him to a wheel-chair. Surely a tragic fate for a man who was prepared to sacrifice his own life to kill Hitler.

The second of these dedicated men was Freiherr Axel von dem Bussche, whom I came to know after the war when he visited us at Garsington with his wife, but I had met a number of his relatives in the past and knew a good deal about him. The von dem Bussches were a Hanoverian military family who over the years had served under the Union Jack and under the Eagle of Germany – but never (as they were proud to point out) under the blue and white standard of Prussia! A von dem Bussche had been a State Secretary in the Foreign Ministry who had opposed the policy of unrestricted U-boat warfare which had been forced upon the Kaiser by Hindenburg and Ludendorff. Another was that unfortunate member of Ludendorff's staff whose melancholy duty it had been in October 1918 to disclose to a meeting of wholly unsuspecting party leaders in the Reichstag the calamitous fact that Germany had lost the war and that terms for an armistice must be sought immediately.

At the outbreak of the Second World War in September 1939 Axel was a young subaltern. Tall, fair-haired, handsome and full of the joy of life, he was yet without hubris, having a generosity of heart and a gallantry of spirit. He served with his regiment in France, in North Africa and later on the Eastern Front, and it was during this period, after the surrender of Stalingrad at the beginning of 1943, that he was initiated into the ranks of the conspiracy. Transferred to duty in Berlin he became a convert to the necessity of killing Hitler rather than arresting him and putting him on trial, and offered himself without flourish or heroics as one who was prepared to give his life in the process.

Though the Wehrmacht had been better prepared in 1942 for the severities and privations of a Russian winter campaign than they had been in the first winter of the war with Russia, which they had fought still wearing the summer uniforms in which they had invaded the Soviet Union in June 1941, there was still room for improvement. In the autumn of 1943, therefore, the army 'boffins' had come up with a design for a new winter overcoat which could by some means or other be proofed against the penetrating, killing cold of Muscovy.

The Führer, ever interested in and careful of such details, had ordered that the garment should be exhibited for his inspection before being officially adopted. Here was an apparently heaven-sent opportunity for action, albeit one requiring courage, daring and self-sacrifice of the highest order. Axel at once came forward with the simplest of plans, but one which marked him as a dedicated assassin. He volunteered to model the overcoat before Hitler, having placed in the pockets some small plastic bombs which would explode on slight contact. He would then grapple with the Führer and they would both perish together.

Some attempts were made to dissuade Axel from this desperate course but he persisted, saying that, in view of the exceedingly strict security precautions with which the Führer surrounded himself, it was only by this means that anyone could get near enough to him to ensure his death. The plan was then accepted and a nerve-racking period ensued, for on every occasion that the demonstration of the overcoat was scheduled to take place the Führer cancelled it, as if through some premonition of extreme danger. Axel's fortitude was, however, proof against this strain and his sincerity of purpose remained unshaken. At last the inspection was fixed for a day in November at the Wehrmacht headquarters at Zossen, a suburb of Berlin.

Axel occupied the preceding night with his final preparations. When morning broke he had made his peace with God and stood ready for his immolation. But neither he nor the Führer were to die that day. A sudden Allied air raid not only completely disrupted the arrangements for the inspection, but also destroyed the supply of the overcoat prototypes. The idea of a repeat performance was abandoned by the leaders of the conspiracy, though Axel protested himself ready and willing to try again. He returned to his regiment on the Eastern Front, thus being in no way implicated in the fiasco of 20 July 1944. Alas, he was wounded very badly in the leg, necessitating amputation, and was invalided out of the army.

It was the failure of 'Operation Overcoat' which brought Claus von Stauffenberg to the forefront of the conspiracy. It was not long before he began to dominate both its thinking and its action, arrogating to himself the exclusive right of the timing and the execution of the *attentat*. Lacking Axel von dem Bussche's dedication and singleness of purpose, he was blessed with no greater success.

Shortly after the unconditional surrender of the German armed forces on 8 May 1945, Axel was brought over to London through the influence of friends and was employed in some consultative capacity by the Foreign Office. It was then that I met him and we became friends. He told me all I know about the abortive 'Operation Overcoat' with a modest simplicity that was remarkable. We also discussed the traumatic experience of having prepared oneself for what seemed to be certain death and then not to die. I realised that it had lefts its mark indelibly upon him, just as I imagine that Lazarus was a permanently changed man after his resurrection.

Axel's courage and his fundamental differentiation between right and wrong remained undaunted. When *The*

Nemesis of Power was finished it created some considerable
controversy in Germany, especially among the former military caste. The German publishing rights were, however,
sold soon after the book's appearance in England and to my
great surprise and admiration I received a request from Axel
that he be allowed to write an introduction, a proposal
which, after warning him of what he might be letting himself in for, I gladly accepted. He was thus precipitated into
the maelstrom of polemics which arose after publication,
and which I fear did him little good.

For a short while he was headmaster of Salem, the recon-
stituted adventurous educational experiment of Kurt Hahn,
and later became head of the German Peace Corps. In 1950
he married Camilla, daughter of the fifth Lord Gosford, who
had previously been the wife of a cousin of Claus von
Stauffenberg; they have three children.

Among my most valuable sources and contacts in the writing
of *The Nemesis of Power* was a man who, though himself
one of the few survivors of the abortive plot of 20 July 1944,
has become the centre of such obloquy and controversy that
his name may well be bracketed with those of Alfred Dreyfus on the one hand, or of Alger Hiss on the other.

Otto John, a Hessian by origin and the son of a civil
servant, was thirty years old at the outbreak of the Second
World War, a qualified lawyer and legal adviser to Lufthansa.
A close friend of the Bonhoeffer family, Dietrich's lawyer
brother Klaus being head of the legal department of Lufthansa, Otto became almost a foundation member of the
resistance movement and, as it were, grew up with it. He
was also a close friend of Prince Louis Ferdinand of Prussia,
another Lufthansa colleague. Otto was initiated into the
military wing of the Opposition by that fine man Colonel
Hans Oster and in due course became an unofficial liaison
channel between the civilians and the soldiers before the
fusing of the two into one general conspiracy.

On the fatal July day Otto was in the Ministry of War in the Bendlerstrasse where the chief conspirators had set up their headquarters. He was present when von Stauffenberg returned from the 'Wolf's Lair' at Rastenburg reporting that Hitler was undoubtedly dead. On the strength of this report Otto left the Bendlerstrasse before the news had come through that the assassination had failed. He returned to his flat and turned on the radio fully expecting to hear General Ludwig Beck's cultured military voice announcing the death of the Führer, the overthrow of the Nazi regime and the establishment of a provisional government with himself as Regent. Instead, however, there came the harsh strident tones of Hitler, proclaiming the fact that he was very much alive and denouncing the conspirators as traitors and enemies of the Reich.

'It was a bad moment,' Otto told me later with a wealth of understatement. Yet he kept his head and went about his business as usual until, three days later, he exercised his privilege as a senior executive to occupy the reserve pilot's seat in a Lufthansa aircraft bound for Madrid. Here he had friends among allied intelligence and through them he was given a visa for Lisbon where, a few days after his arrival, he was arrested and lodged as a political prisoner in the mediaeval fortress of Aljube. This action on the part of the Portuguese authorities, taken on a tip from the British embassy who were aware of the dangers which beset him, while depriving Otto of freedom undoubtedly saved his life, for while he was thus interned the odds were against his being arrested and taken back to Germany. The long arm of Himmler's revenge stretched as far as Lisbon whither he had despatched a special Gestapo detachment, as a result of whose activities more than one of those suspected of making contact with the British embassy were returned to Berlin in trunks considerately addressed to their next of kin.

It had been easy to get the Portuguese government to intern Otto but it was much more difficult to persuade them to release him. He had been offered to the Political Intelligence Department of the Foreign Office – of my association with which I have written in *Special Relationships* – as a possible asset for our 'black' propaganda to Germany. Bruce Lockhart had sounded out Tom Delmer, the head of our 'black' activities to Germany, and had received an enthusiastic reaction: we were anxious to get hold of him. At last a signal came through that he was to be flown to Poole from Lisbon on a certain date in September and would we meet him. A representative of the department was despatched to Poole and I well remember our chagrin and dismay when the report came through that no contact had been made. Otto had simply vanished into thin air. Was it possible, we wondered, that Himmler had caught up with him at last?

Happily this was not the case, and our quarry was located in one of those strange institutions called 'Patriotic Schools' where defectors and other foreigners entering the country in an unusual manner were investigated and interrogated. In Otto's case the circumstances had been complicated by the fact that in order to disguise himself his hair, usually blond, had been dyed – and it must be confessed not too expertly – with boot-blacking, so that instead of presenting his usual very agreeable appearance of a good-looking, fair-haired, pink-and-white young man, he looked like a somewhat comically disguised character in a French farce. This in itself was enough to arouse the suspicions of Security!

Tom Delmer, on behalf of our department, eventually rescued Otto from his dilemma. By this time he had washed the blacking out of his hair but had gone to the other extreme of applying a peroxide preparation, which gave the effect of a brassy brightness.

Tom was appalled, for he had already been sent as a recruit a German diplomat who wore long silk stockings! 'Good God, not another of *those*,' was his first reaction. But Otto soon dispelled his fears as to his normality. The two became excellent friends and Otto proved a valuable asset to Tom's outfit.

(I remember a similar hirsute problem arising when that gallant old veteran of the French Right, Louis Marin, made his escape to this country. He was well known in public life as a figure with flowing grey locks, a voluminous blue polka-dot cravat, and a heavy white moustache. In order to avoid attention he dyed his hair black, abandoned the cravat and shaved off the moustache, and it was in this unrecognisable condition that he was met, not without some difficulty, by a bewildered member of the Foreign Office.)

It was now in the last months of the war that I first met Otto John. Though I was not directly concerned with the 'black' side of our work, it was sometimes necessary for me to go to Woburn and he occasionally came to London. I found him at once *gemütlich* and possessed of a delightful sense of humour, but he was still a victim to the inevitable depression of one who has survived a period of despair, in which not only many of his friends (some of whom were mine also) but also his much loved brother Hans had been executed for 'treason'. We had both friends and ideas in common, and our talks inevitably turned to the future of Germany in which both of us were interested. From the first Otto feared that, after a short period of 'going to ground', the ex-Nazis would reappear as respectable citizens of the new German state and would even find their way back into government employment. His conviction was a source of deep concern to him. Like myself, he was desperately anxious that the spirit of militarism and the influence of the armed forces should never again establish their ascendancy within Germany.

However, his periods of depression were varied and relieved by romance. Through a female colleague of his at Woburn he had met her mother, Lucie Manen, a lady of Jewish descent, who had achieved considerable distinction in the European operatic world, who had come over to sing at Glyndebourne with Fritz Busch in 1934 and had settled in London. Otto often visited her flat in Hampstead. The two fell in love and were married in December 1949. Lucie has subsequently embarked on a second and highly successful career in the field of voice production, in which she has attained an international reputation.

After the conclusion of hostilities on V.E. day, Otto was recruited by the British element of the Control Council for Germany to interrogate in depth the inmates of a very high grade prisoner-of-war camp at Bridgend in South Wales. Here were gathered together several hundred former German field-marshals, generals, admirals and senior S.S. officers. Some of them responded willingly to his questioning. Others despised him as a British stooge. This was, in a sense, the beginning of his later tragedy, which epitomised the profound difficulty confronting so many Germans in the difference of their interpretation of the word 'patriotism'.

When I began my preliminary researches for *The Nemesis of Power* Otto proved an invaluable asset – over and above the normal demands of friendship. Not only did he write for me a long and detailed memorandum of the background of the conspiracy which terminated so disastrously on 20 July 1944, but it was thanks to him that I met many of those who had been involved in the plot though not in the holocaust in the Bendlerstrasse.

Lucie and Otto came to stay with us at Garsington on several occasions, and during my periodic visits to Western Germany I met such varied characters as Prince Louis Ferdinand of Prussia, who told me much about his contacts with the conspirators, and their eventually unanimous decision that the new Germany must be a monarchy with himself as sovereign; Jacob Kaiser, who was to have been Vice-Chancellor in Goerdeler's provisional government; Joseph Müller (nicknamed *Ochsensepp*, or Joe the Ox, from his fine physique), the Bavarian lawyer who had negotiated on behalf of the conspirators in 1940 with Pope Pius XII and the

British Minister to the Holy See, Sir D'Arcy Osbourne (later the last Duke of Leeds); and the two sons, Ludwig and Konrad, of General Kurt von Hammerstein, whom I had known as small boys playing in the garden of their father's house in the Berlin suburb of Zehlendorf, when I used to visit him there before the Nazi revolution.

Colonel-General Freiherr Kurt von Hammerstein-Equord, of Hanoverian military stock, was G.O.C. of the Reichswehr during the last days of the Weimar Republic and the advent of Hitler. He was a man of courage, principle and personal integrity and enjoyed the confidence and loyalty of his troops. In the last madly contorted moments of General von Schleicher's Chancellorship, he had proposed a plan for the arrest by the Reichswehr of President von Hindenburg and his son Oskar, Franz von Papen and General von Blomberg, and the setting up of a military junta to govern the country. Exactly what was to be the relationship of Hitler to this body was never made clear, and in any case von Schleicher had by that time become so devoid of initiative that he would neither agree nor dissent. Precious hours were lost and the Hammerstein Plot never developed. He remained loyal to von Schleicher, however, and after the latter's murder on the Night of the Long Knives, von Hammerstein not only attended his funeral in full uniform but also headed the movement for his rehabilitation, which Hitler was later compelled to concede though he dismissed Hammerstein shortly thereafter. Until his death in April 1943, the General remained an implacable opponent of the Nazi regime and a venerated leader of the conspiracy.

I had known Kurt von Hammerstein well until 1934 and had admired him. We had often discussed the dilemma which confronted many of the senior members of the Officer Corps at that time and he had spoken very frankly. He was in many ways the epitome of the best in the German military tradition and, although I could never understand nor approve his loyalty to Kurt von Schleicher,

I could not but respect it. At the request of Otto John, his son Konrad prepared a very valuable memorandum for me based upon the General's papers, which had been hidden after his death, giving a detailed account of his activities before Hitler's coming to power and of his subsequent participation in the conspiracy. It is now in the custody of St Antony's College, Oxford, together with Otto's own.

Otto and I both assisted the prosecution at the trial of Field-Marshal Erich von Manstein before a British court martial at Hamburg during the autumn of 1949. It was a bizarre affair in every way. To begin with, the accused as a Field-Marshal was entitled to be tried by his peers and consequently to have at least one member of the court of equal rank. However, no British Field-Marshals were forthcoming and, there being no volunteers from among the general officers of the army, Lieutenant-General Sir Frank Simpson (then, I think, G.O.C. Southern Command) was ordered to preside over a court largely composed, as I recall, of brigadiers.

The British people were bored to death with war-crimes trials and there was ironically enough a general sympathy for von Manstein who, though he was a fine, even a brilliant, soldier, had been, when I knew him in Berlin as a colonel, one of the most disliked members of the Officer Corps. Now, however, a fund was raised, to which Sir Winston Churchill made a contribution, to provide him with the services of a British lawyer for his defence. The choice fell upon Mr Reginald Paget, who had a colourful career both as a Q.C. and as a Labour Member of Parliament. It was a typically British sporting instinct which prompted this gesture: von Manstein had had an outstanding war record and many German officers considered him their most illustrious strategist. At any rate he had proved himself an opponent worthy of our steel, albeit it was chiefly Russian steel, and we should therefore demonstrate our sense of fair play by assisting him in his defence, despite the fact that he was to be tried before a British military court.

In point of fact, the Field-Marshal already had at his disposal two of the leading members of the German bar, Dr Hans Laternser, who had already made a first-class performance in defence of the German General Staff at Nuremberg, and Dr Paul Leverkuhn of Hamburg. The result of this curious legal amalgam was not wholly felicitous. There was little love lost between Paget and Laternser, nor between the latter and von Manstein.

The prosecution was led by Sir Arthur Comyns-Carr together with Elwyn Jones, an old friend of mine from Nuremberg days. Again, a bitter antipathy developed between Paget and Comyns-Carr, which resulted on several occasions, two of which I witnessed, in an unseemly dispute over the use of the microphone, involving much shoving and jockeying for position. It would have been farcical had it not been so damaging to the dignity of the Court, despite all General Simpson's efforts to maintain some modicum of decorum, while von Manstein sat alone in the dock, cold and aloof and contemptuous.

Frank Simpson was unhappy about the whole thing and used to ask me to dine with him in his suite in the Four Seasons Hotel, the former occupants of which had included both Kaiser Wilhelm II and Adolf Hitler. He used to ask me questions about the German army, and was greatly interested when I talked about the book I was writing on this subject. He was very helpful in opening up the archives of the court to me.

I also spent several evenings with Comyns-Carr, who was at the close of a long career which had embraced many fascinating legal battles. Tall, thin and acerbic, he was a splendid raconteur and held me riveted with the story of how he had routed the seemingly invincible Horatio Bottomley, who had so often conducted his own defence with conspicuous success.

Bottomley, once a name to conjure with, now perhaps almost forgotten, was an extraordinary blend of patriot and swindler, politician and rogue. As a member of the House of Commons during the war (and re-elected in the Khaki Election of 1918) he rubbed shoulders with Lloyd George, Bonar Law and Winston Churchill. He was accounted one of the greatest orators of his day in England, and could pack Trafalgar Square and the Albert Hall for recruiting meetings from which many young men went to join the colours while the sale of war bonds boomed appreciably. Indeed it was the sale of Victory Bonds that led to his ultimate undoing. His weekly paper *John Bull* – a scurrilous rag if ever there was one – harped continuously upon the patriotic note and blasted not a few reputations in the process.

It is no part of my story to follow Horatio Bottomley through the intricate maze of his nefarious career. Suffice it to say that he and Comyns-Carr had met before in various legal actions and that the latter's greatest forensic triumph was when he paved the way for Bottomley's final fall. Comyns-Carr was hard-bitten and stern in appearance, with a slight Irish accent which he used to advantage. In the course of a long career in both civil and criminal law he had acquired a reputation for boldness and persistency in the conduct of cases, fearing neither judges nor eminent opponents, and had become a justly feared master in the art of cross-examination.

Comyns-Carr's triumph over Bottomley arose from charges of criminal libel and attempts to obtain money by menaces which Bottomley brought against one Reuben Bigland, who had denounced him as 'a common swindler' in connection with his misconduct of the affairs of the Victory Bonds Club which he had founded. The case opened at Bow Street on 8 October 1921, before Sir Chartres Biron, with Comyns-Carr appearing for Bigland. Under his ruthless and tenacious cross-examination, against the severity of which Bottomley several times appealed for the protection of the court, even threatening to report his opponent to Bar Council, Bottomley was shown to be a deliberate perjurer. His accusation of menaces against Bigland completely broke down, and this charge was dismissed. On the libel charge Sir Chartres Biron had no option but to commit Bigland for trial, but as a result of the subsequent proceedings Bottomley was totally discredited and ultimately found himself on trial in May of the following year at the Old Bailey, indicted for the misappropriation of the Victory Bonds Club funds. Despite his dramatic conduct of his own defence, which included bursting into tears, he could not escape conviction and a sentence of seven years' penal servitude.

With all this Arthur Comyns-Carr regaled me in Hamburg, with a wealth of detail which, I am sure, lost nothing in the telling. Although he had not been concerned with the Old Bailey trial, he was at pains to draw my attention to the high tribute which Sir Chartres Biron pays in his book, *Without Prejudice*, to Comyns-Carr's conduct of the Bow Street proceedings which had destroyed Horatio Bottomley's image and credibility.

At other times during our talks together Comyns-Carr would delight me with waspish anecdotes of the war crimes trials in Tokyo before the International Military Tribunal for the Far East, at which he had been leader of the British prosecution team. From his account it would appear that moments of shambles – as for example when one member of the court had to retire temporarily to recover from the effects of severe alcoholism – had alternated with periods of extreme boredom. The trials had lasted for nearly three years and often the recital of the vastly crowded period of Oriental history became, despite its horrors and its infamy, extremely tedious. Not infrequently, as Comyns-Carr freely admitted, the wrangling of the attendant legal luminaries seemed pettifogging and picayune, and it was clear to me from his reminiscences that the Tokyo proceedings had lacked the dignity and masterly British predominance, as well as the despatch, of the Nuremberg Tribunal.

To return to Hamburg: Manstein was eventually acquitted on the majority of the charges brought against him, but his conviction on the remainder brought him a sentence of eighteen years' imprisonment.

Mr Paget, in his naturally somewhat predisposed book, *Manstein, his Campaigns and his Trial*, takes full credit for the whittling down of the Field-Marshal's convictions, and records that, after the conclusion of his closing speech, Manstein took his hand and, weeping freely, said, 'You who were my enemy have taken years of bitterness from my heart,' and added, 'This has been a lovely birthday.' He was sixty-two on that day. It must have been an affecting scene.

He served only four years of his sentence, during which time he was visited in prison by the Federal Chancellor. Thereafter he emerged to enjoy the not inconsiderable pension of a field-marshal granted to him by the Adenauer administration. He died in 1973.

In 1949 and 1950 Otto John was faced with making certain fateful decisions which were to have tragic results in the years ahead. It was open to him to remain in Britain and complete his qualifications for practising commercial law in this country, a prospect which had always rather appealed to him. It was even made known to him that, should he desire it, the process of his nationalisation to British citizenship could be accelerated and both Lord Vansittart and I had offered to act as his sponsors.

Otto was torn between the comparatively peaceful, and in time even profitable, career thus presented and what his other self demanded of him as his patriotic duty, namely to return to Germany and play some part in building up the new state which was gradually emerging from the amalgamation of the British, American and French zones of occupation. On 23 May 1949 the West German Federal Republic came into being with its capital in Bonn, and, though it did not enjoy complete national sovereignty, many of the responsibilities of the occupying authorities were transferred to it and further concessions were made in the Petersburg Agreement of the following November. Theodor Heuss became the first Federal President, but from then until his retirement in 1959 – and indeed until his death some four years later – the dominant figure in German politics was the first *Bundeskanzler*, Konrad Adenauer.

When Otto told me toward the end of 1949 of his decision to return to Germany, resume his citizenship and his legal practice and, if called upon, enter the service of the Republic, I was gravely disturbed, but this was nothing to my horror at his announcement a few months later of the job he had been offered and accepted. The story of his brief period of office and its tragic, crucifying sequel, has been told by Otto himself with poignant restraint in his book, *Twice through the Lines*, and with more verve and righteous wrath by Tom Delmer in *Black Boomerang*. I do not intend to repeat it here except in so far as I was peripherally involved.

I had planned to meet Otto in Bonn towards the end of October 1950 for a further series of interviews, and he had mentioned this fact to President Heuss, with whom, as an old family friend of Lucie John, Otto was on familiar terms. I had known Heuss fairly well in the Weimar days, when he had been a member of the Democratic Party in the Reichstag, and had always enjoyed his company, for he liked good food and drink and surrounded himself with people of interest. He was a patriot and a man of great personal probity, having strong principles which made it impossible for him to associate with the Nazi Party. Though his party had voted for the passing of the Enabling Act in March 1933, Heuss's books had been among those publicly burned in the triumphant vandalism of the S.A. Since we had last seen one another he had read my books and approved of them and he now asked Otto to bring me to see him so that we might renew our old relationship.

Thus it was that at ten o'clock on Thursday, 26 October, Otto and I called at the villa on the Venusberg which had become the temporary residence of the *Bundespräsident* until he moved into the Palais Hammerschmidt. Heuss had changed very little with the years. He was greyer, of course, and stooped a little, but he had retained his pleasing sense of humour, his dignity and his courteous kindliness. After he had greeted me he asked if he might be excused for a brief word alone with Otto and they went off to the other end of the long reception room. I could see that their conversation was a short exchange of question and answer, and as they came down the room to rejoin me I heard the President say to Otto, 'Very important, very important. We must ensure that we don't have another 1933.' Then he turned to me and we had a pleasant hour with memories of old days in Berlin, some mutually tactful references to the war and some interesting comments on his part on how the course of world events (by which he meant the cold war) had greatly accelerated the process of restoring German national sovereignty. 'We should not have gone half as far half as quickly if it had not been for the Russians,' he said. We parted with an exchange of our inscribed works. He gave me his *1848, Werk und Erbe* and I responded with a copy of *Hindenburg*.

There were two sequels to this agreeable experience, one immediate and not entirely pleasurable, had it not been so humorous, the second more long-term and wholly pleasing, if unexpected. So informal had been our visit and on such friendly terms that Otto had arranged it personally with Heuss on the telephone, thereby bypassing the head of the President's protocol department, an act which earned him the enmity of that outraged official; while I for my part, in the pleasure of a reunion with an old friend, had completely forgotten the point of etiquette which prohibits a private individual from calling on a chief of state without having previously informed his embassy. Ivone Kirkpatrick, our High Commissioner, was on leave but Kit Steel, his Deputy, though an old friend, was furious, and administered an official 'wigging' through which I sat barely able to keep a straight face, because, though I sincerely regretted what was undoubtedly an act of discourtesy, though obviously entirely unintentional, his sense of affront and the ferocity of his rebuke seemed really rather disproportionate to the offence. However, having blown off steam and listened to my explanations and apologies (which he had given me no opportunity to express earlier!), he relented and we had a drink together.

The second sequel was longer delayed. When President Heuss made his ill-advised and premature state visit to London in October 1958 the Foreign Office gave a reception in Lancaster House at which the Queen and Prince Philip and President Heuss and his wife were present. Ruth and I were also invited and it was a delight to see the glittering splendour and effortless dignity with which the British stage-manage their state occasions. As the procession passed up the great hall to a dais, the President suddenly caught sight of me and, somewhat, I think, to the Queen's surprise, beamed charmingly and waved his hand in the most friendly manner. On the following day I got a request from the German embassy to go to Buckingham Palace where I was received by the President in the Belgian Suite. It was nice of him, I thought, to spare fifteen minutes in the very crowded schedule of a state visit to talk to me.

To return, however, to the occasion of my visit to Heuss in October 1950. That evening Otto John and I dined together and he told me that he had been offered the appointment of Head of the Federal Office for Protection of the Constitution (*Bundesamt für Verfassungsschutz*), that is, internal security, and it had been the importance of this task to which the President had referred so emphatically at the conclusion of their brief exchange that morning. Otto went on to say that after consultation with Jacob Kaiser, then Minister of All-German Affairs, he had accepted the position.

I was aghast. My poor friend, I felt, had walked into a political quicksand which would gradually engulf him. He was so tragically, so pathetically, vulnerable. In the Germany that was emerging the old establishment, the former military caste and certain ex-Nazis were booming on the market of the new national chauvinism and correspondingly the survivors of the conspiracy of 20 July 1944 were at a discount. The Federal Attorney-General, Dr Max Guede, made the position clear on a memorable occasion when he stated: 'The dead of 20 July are people we must honour, but the survivors should not be boastful. Honour belongs to the dead alone.'

To all these categories Otto John was anathema. He was a survivor of 20 July; he had worked with the British for the defeat of Germany; he had interrogated, again on the part of the British, some of the highest ranking members of the German armed services when they were prisoners of war; he had assisted the prosecution at the trial of Field-Marshal von Manstein, regarded as the *preux chevalier*, the paladin of honour, by the younger members of the officer corps. Notable among these was General Reinhard Gehlen, one of von Manstein's personal protégés, who had been Hitler's Chief of Intelligence against the Russians and had as early as 1947 transferred himself, together with his whole organization, to the protection of the Americans.

All these groups had their representatives in high places who could be calculated to obstruct, frustrate and ultimately eliminate Otto. Thus both Dr Hans Globke, author of the notorious legal commentary on the infamous Nuremberg anti-semitic laws, and General Gehlen had direct access to Adenauer himself, and the General succeeded in getting one of his own ex-staff officers appointed as Otto's deputy.

Then there was the Chancellor himself. Konrad Adenauer entertained a personal aversion toward Otto John because of the latter's unswerving opposition to Hitler and for his 'higher patriotism'. This had not been entirely the record of the 'Old Fox'. Having been dismissed by the Nazis in 1933 from his office of Oberbürgermeister of Cologne, he wrote to Wilhelm Frick, Hitler's Minister of the Interior, in August 1934 applying for compensation for deprivation of office and the grant of a pension, and citing in support of his case the services he had rendered to the National Socialist Party before they took power, in defiance of directives from the Reich Government and of the Centre Party, of which he had been a member and also President of the Prussian State Council. A copy of this letter is in the West German Central Archives.* Ten years later, as his official biographer records, he had vehemently declined an invitation from Karl Goerdeler to join the provisional government which the conspirators were then forming. All this was known to Otto John, and Adenauer knew that he knew. It did not make for better relations.

Against such a powerful combination of forces it seemed to me that Otto had no chance of success. Knowing from my experience of the Weimar Republic the infinite capacity of Germans in politics for intrigue and counter-intrigue, for character assassination and the denigration of reputations, there was a hideous sense of *déjà vu* about the whole situation. How often had I seen the destruction of men of integrity and honour by the machinations of such persons as von Schleicher and Hugenberg? It was horrifying that Otto should risk his whole career in this manner. I begged him to reconsider, or at least defer, his acceptance of so sensitive and exposed an office, and, when he persisted, I hoped against hope that the Allied High Commissioners, who, since Germany was as yet only a semi-sovereign state, had the power to veto or confirm all such appointments, might decide

*Deutsches Zentralarchiv, Abfe : Iung Merseburg. Ref. 77, Pilf. 444, Nr. 3. Band 10, Beiheft, Blatt 155–156. Quoted by Sefton Delmer, *Black Boomerang* (London, 1962) p. 276.

against Otto. But there was no real hope of this. While Otto John was certainly not Adenauer's favourite candidate for the new post, neither was he by any means the first. The Chancellor had canvassed at least a dozen earlier choices. Some of them had declined and others who had accepted had been rejected by the High Commissioners as unsuitable or unreliable. There could be no such objection to Otto's record and his appointment was unanimously approved.

It was two years before I made my next, and incidentally, my last visit to Germany, in the summer of 1952. Ruth and I stayed first at Cologne with Lucie and Otto and then went on to Ivone and Violet Kirkpatrick at Wahn. While Lucie and Ruth made a motor tour down the Rhine to Lake Constance, I remained behind, partly to make some final checks before sending *Nemesis* to my publishers and partly to talk with Otto. I found him perceptibly aged and both nervous and depressed. He was showing signs of strain and complained that, besides being surrounded by his enemies, he was isolated from many of his friends and that Ivone Kirkpatrick would hold no relations with him. Later, when we were staying at Wahn, I asked Ivone about this and he gave two fairly cogent answers. At the outset he had been at some pains to avoid Otto in order not to give weight to the charge of his being a British agent which was constantly being levelled against him. Then, after the signature of the Contractual Agreement in May 1952, by which full sovereignty was restored to the government of the West German Republic, he had even less excuse or reason to have relations with the head of the Security Service (the equivalent of MI5) of a foreign power.

Indeed the restoration of sovereignty had greatly weakened Otto's position. He was now deprived of the protection of the High Commissioners and could be dismissed at the order of the Chancellor. He fully expected, he said, that this would happen at any moment. He told me in no uncertain terms of the increase of influence which former Nazis and ex-members of the old military caste were exercising in the formulation of policy, and expressed considerable concern as to what the effect would be of Germany's rearmament in accordance with her membership of the European Defence Community (or, as it turned out to be, the Western European Union). Though Otto was, as ever, a charming and excellent host, and after Lucie and Ruth returned to Cologne we found much to laugh over, I left with the impression that he was a very unhappy man.

Again two years passed. I had finished *Nemesis* and was deeply involved in my early research for the writing of King George VI's life. On the afternoon of 22 July 1954, I came down to Garsington without having seen the evening papers. I found waiting on the doorstep a stranger who identified himself as the representative of a great national newspaper. 'You are, I believe, a friend of Dr Otto John's,' he said, and seemed to wait expectantly for my reply. I said that this was correct. Realising that I was unaware of the reason for his visit, he stated bluntly: 'He has just absconded to the Soviet sector of Berlin and has announced his intention of staying there.'

I was stunned by the news, but from the first I felt deep in my heart that more, much more, lay beneath this original but perfectly factual statement. Otto *had* entered the Soviet sector and he *had* made a statement of his intention to stay there. This, however, was after attending a reunion of the survivors of the July conspiracy and their relations on the tenth anniversary of the plot, when a memorial tablet had been unveiled in the courtyard of the old Ministry of War in the Bendlerstrasse, in which Claus von Stauffenberg and some of his comrades had been summarily executed on that fatal evening. It must, I thought, have been a tragically emotional affair, and it would not have surprised me if Otto had reacted strangely to the effect of sad memories thus evoked. However, leaving aside the whole cloak-and-dagger elements of the case which subsequently emerged, I was very sure that he had not defected nor was he a Communist agent. I said this to my visiting journalist, and nothing which has subsequently occurred has caused me to change my mind. I also gave him some of my reasons. In many talks which I had had with Otto he made very little difference between his attitude to the Nazis and his attitude to the Communists. He hated both and despised tyranny. Indeed, he was at heart a romantic, even a sentimental, monarchist – due in no small measure to his friendship with Prince Louis Ferdinand of Prussia – but first of all he was a loyal German patriot. Whatever his feelings against his political opponents in the West German Federal Republic may have been, he would never have exchanged his position there for any which the People's Democratic Republic of Germany could offer him. Indeed, had he wished to shake the dust of Western Germany off his feet, he would have been much more likely to have made a break for Britain. Moreover he was completely reconciled to a divided Germany, whereas at that time reunification was the hard party line dictated from Moscow. I still believe this.

There followed eighteen months in which my unfortunate friend was kept in varying degrees of detentive severity in East Berlin, Moscow and the Crimea, during which time he was interrogated almost continuously. Then suddenly in December 1955 he contrived, or was allowed, to cross into West Berlin and at once gave himself up to the authorities. A year later he was brought to trial on charges that he, as a person entrusted with the highest German state secrets, had entered into relations with the Russians and East German authorities which were suspected of having been treasonable.

When the trial closed on 22 December 1956, the leader of the prosecution had failed to make good his indictments against Otto John that he was a Communist agent or that he had betrayed secrets, since it had been proved that no agents had been arrested as a result of any communication which he had made to the Russians, and these charges had been dropped. However, the Attorney-General stuck to his accusation of 'treasonable conspiracy' and asked for a sentence of two years' imprisonment. The court found him guilty as charged, and on its own initiative doubled the sentence demanded by the prosecution. Under German justice there is no appeal from this Federal Court. Otto served his full time in prison, less a remission for good conduct.

On completing his sentence in July 1958 Otto at once set about the task of clearing his name. Ill fortune has dogged his efforts, but he has lost none of his courage or his determination. Now living in Austria, he accumulates new evidence and delights in the success of his wife. He is also sustained by his friends. In addition to Lucie's noble loyalty, Prince Louis Ferdinand stood bravely by him, and Tom Delmer succeeded in visiting him in East Berlin and later appeared at his trial as an effective witness for the defence. I did what I could when the occasion arose and am gratified that, in sending me a copy of his book, he inscribed it 'with heartiest thanks for a friendship which never wavered'. We meet and dine together whenever he comes to London.

In concluding his introduction to the English edition of Otto's book, Hugh Trevor-Roper has written of 'the authority which Dr John, by his own civil courage, is entitled to claim. His is the voice of a European who refused to minister to his own comfort by despairing of Europe.' There could be no fairer assessment of his character.

The Nemesis of Power was published in the autumn of 1953 and was well received both in Britain and America. Some years later, in reading the third volume of Harold Nicolson's *Diaries*, I was gratified to find the following entry for 11 January 1954: 'I finish Jack Wheeler-Bennett's book *Nemesis of Power*. It really is a magnificent work.'

The book was translated into a number of languages (including Japanese) but, alas, not this time into Russian.

Indeed, in company with the works of Alan Bullock and Hugh Trevor-Roper, *Nemesis* was banned by the Soviet authorities from the British Book Exhibition in Moscow in November 1959! (Of this incident Hugh Trevor-Roper is reported as saying that 'the Russians made fools of themselves by banning the three best books which have been written on Germany since the war.') It was not entirely surprising to me that when the German edition appeared in 1954 it almost immediately became the centre of controversy, and Axel von dem Bussche's courageous introduction did little to pour oil on the eristic waters. To some Germans the book was a revelation; to others a jolt to their memories and consciences; in others again it evoked execration in that it laid to some degree a profane hand upon the sacrosanct record of the *Generalität* as it was affected by politics.

It also came to me from reliable sources both inside and outside Germany that the book exercised a not inconsiderable influence on the thinking of those who were at that moment engaged in building up the new *Bundeswehr* in Western Germany and were anxious to avoid the mistakes which had been made during the Weimar Republic in the relations between the government and the army.

Whatever the value *Nemesis* may or may not have had, its reception could not be said to be apathetic.

Very shortly after the book had appeared I became deeply involved in the research preliminary to the writing of the life of King George VI, the story of which I shall tell in the final chapter of this volume. This biography appeared in 1959, and shortly thereafter Macmillan decided to bring out a second edition of *The Nemesis of Power*. In doing so, however, they very properly desired me to take into consideration the large quantity of additional supplementary evidence which appeared in Germany in memoirs and in documentary form during the years since the book was originally published. Though there was nothing in this new material which would change one way or the other my general conclusions, there were corroborative details which in certain cases filled gaps in the original edition and of which cognizance must be taken.

I was exhausted after six years' work on the King's life and also not in very good health. To plunge again into the field of German politics was a daunting prospect and one on which I did not think I could embark single-handed.

As I have done frequently – and never without success – I turned for aid and succour to my old friend Bill (now Sir William) Deakin, then Warden of St Antony's College, of which at his invitation I had become a founding Fellow in 1950. Could he, I asked, provide me with a research assistant who could do the preparatory work for my second edition? 'I think I've got just the chap for you,' he said. 'He's a Research Fellow of ours called Tony Nicholls. His field is modern German history, he's a hard worker and very accurate and above all he's an extremely nice person. I'll send him out to Garsington to see you.'

In due course Tony came and both Ruth and I took to him immediately. Apart from the fact that all that Bill had said of him was true, he had our sense of humour and from the word go we found ourselves laughing. I have never made a wiser decision in my career as a historian than when I formed a partnership with Tony Nicholls, and I have always been deeply grateful to Bill Deakin for bringing it about. Tony was well informed in the background of the period and knew exactly how to set about the work at hand. It was not only most pleasurable but also most salutary for me to get the reactions of a younger man – Tony was under thirty when I first knew him – with an historian's perspective toward personalities and events which I had known at first hand. Moreover, we soon found that we not only shared an historical interest and a sense of humour but also that our literary styles were – for better, for worse – almost identical. As we worked together we developed a common and almost indistinguishable manner of writing which was invaluable for our present purpose and was to prove a great asset in the future. By the time we had brought the second edition of *Nemesis* to birth in 1963, Tony (and later his charming wife Christine) had become very much a part of our family.

Not quite two years later we were to be in double harness again. One advantage of Garsington is that it is within striking distance of Oxford and one of the happiest consequences for Ruth and myself of Harold Macmillan's election as Chancellor of the University has been the fact that we not infrequently have the great pleasure of his presence in our house. No one could be a more welcome guest nor a more entertaining companion.

It was during one of these visits, some time in the summer of 1964, that the three of us were perambulating round the garden when Harold turned to me with the question, 'What are you going to write now?' I replied indefinitely that I had been thinking of doing a slim volume on Philip Lothian's ambassadorship in Washington at the beginning of the war, during which time I had been his Personal Assistant. Harold brushed this aside with the air of one who dismisses a handful of small change. 'That will come later,' he said. 'But you must write one more major work before you die.'

Somewhat startled by this abrupt confrontation with the imminence of death and feeling that I must already have one foot in the grave, I capitulated to his commands with even more than my usual alacrity. Indeed I at once consulted him on what subject he would suggest that I write. Harold is never at a loss for an answer. Without batting an eyelid he replied, 'Why don't you write the history of the political settlement after the Second World War?' The idea appealed to me at once and I promised to think it over seriously.

This was an intimidating assignment, and on reflection I speedily reached the conclusion that it was too big a project, requiring too vast an amount of research, for me to tackle single-handed. So, after further consideration, I asked Tony Nicholls, whom I regard as one of the most outstanding of the younger modern historians at Oxford, if he would come in with me as co-author of the book and to my great delight he agreed to do so. Thus began a five-year partnership which was, I believe, a period of enjoyment for both of us. We were completely complementary and we worked together in the greatest consonance and amity. It was interesting to find that though we often approached specific subjects from different angles we almost always arrived at the same conclusions.

We read what seemed to be thousands of documents and personal papers; we laboured through scores of memoirs, diaries and biographies; we talked with dozens of persons who had participated in one way or another in the events we had under review. We began with Mr Chamberlain's bewildering broadcast to the German people on 4 September 1939, in which he announced that Britain had no quarrel with them but only with their masters, and followed the story of the development of the peace settlement through its many vicissitudes and complexities to the formation of the North Atlantic Alliance, the Western European Union and the Warsaw Pact. Our method was to divide up between us the various periods, exchanging drafts and comments on each other's work, and the fact that our style of writing was strangely similar resulted in the majority of our readers being unable to distinguish who had written which chapters.

The book, entitled *The Semblance of Peace*, was published in November 1970 and had the satisfactory outcome of piquing the professional pundits, enraging revisionists of the New Left and earning commendation from those quarters whence approval was most appreciated both in Britain and America. The *Times Literary Supplement*, that paragon of illustrious criticism, was good enough to describe it as 'a distinguished study'.

CHAPTER FIVE

Biographer Royal

When I was in Egypt in 1927 I made the acquaintance of a somewhat disreputable old character who combined the callings of snake-charmer and astrologer. His snake-charming abilities, which were considerable, were subsequently to have an impact on my academic career, but it is his astrological prognoses that have at least an indirect bearing upon the subject of this chapter.

Having supplied him with the necessary data – day, date and hour of birth and so on – I was presented a few days later with a rather grubby piece of paper on which, written in very pidgin English, were a series of predictions, which, though they sounded fantastically unbelievable to me then, have in the main been fulfilled. Among them was the statement that I should write of kings, serve in the business of kings and receive high honour in that service.

But I was five-and-twenty when this incident occurred and I put little faith in prophecy.

On the morning of 6 February 1952 I was sitting in my room at the Foreign Office annexe on the South Bank when something prompted me to look out of the window. It looked over the Thames and had a wide view of other government buildings. Suddenly, as if by some simultaneous command, I saw the flags everywhere lowered to half-mast. I rang the switch-board to enquire the reason: the King of England was dead.

In the previous autumn King George had undergone a serious operation for cancer of the lung, an operation on which his life had hung in the balance. His illness had been the occasion of widespread concern throughout the world and his recovery one of universal rejoicing. Day after day, often in gloom and drizzle, silent crowds had waited outside Buckingham Palace for word of their Sovereign. Their mute patience was in itself an eloquent witness to their solicitude.

But the King had weathered the danger, seemingly with moderate triumph. He was admittedly frail, but by the close of the year his recovery was well advanced, and on the morning of 31 January, hatless and wind-blown, he had waved good-bye to Princess Elizabeth and Prince Philip at London Airport as they departed on the first stage of a Commonwealth visit.

Now he was dead and all England was stunned. Within an hour London had donned its mourning. A tie, a scarf, an arm-band, a cloak or dress all bore honour to the national loss. Shops dressed their windows accordingly, though in Bond Street it amounted in one case to a display of black lingerie. The people of England made no secret of the depth and sincerity of their sorrow. I saw many in tears.

A week later, on the bitterly cold morning of 15 February, Ruth and I and a party of friends watched the royal funeral procession from a window of the Ritz. We saw the slow march of the troops, heard the bands of the Brigade of Guards play the Dead March from *Saul* and Chopin's Funeral March, and the soughing of the Highland piper's lament. The great ones of the world, Europe, America and the Commonwealth, passed before us, and the three veiled mourning queens – two royal widows and the young Sovereign.

A royal funeral is something of especial emotional quality, when a nation stands silent and united in one common bond of loss and sorrow. I have seen three of them in London, those of King Edward VII, King George V and King George VI, and I was in Brussels when King Albert of the Belgians returned for the last time to his capital, by torchlight in the shadows of the evening. Deeply moving though it is, profoundly cleansing to the soul, I pray I may never see another.

The spring and summer of 1952 passed quietly and on the week-end of 15 August Harold and Vita Nicolson came to stay with us in Oxfordshire. Harold was, of course, an old friend. We had first met in Berlin in 1926 when he was chargé d'affaires at the embassy and we had been associated thereafter pretty closely during the Munich Crisis and throughout the war. I saw him frequently and Ruth and I were often with him at his chambers in Albany.

With Vita we were less well acquainted. She had a reputation for formidable intellectual detachment and was an authority on gardening, writing an erudite weekly column in the *Sunday Times*. I had only met her once and Ruth never. I was therefore somewhat surprised when Harold buttonholed me at one of our clubs and confided that neither he nor she had ever seen Garsington; they longed to do so, and might they spend a week-end with us. I relayed this message to Ruth and, with some trepidation on our part, a date was set. Ruth was daunted by the fact that in one of her recent columns Vita had decried the use of annuals in summer gardens and at the moment our flowerbeds were gay with them. Nor was our apprehension lessened by a further communication from Harold. 'I just want to warn you,' he said to me, 'that Vita is terribly shy. She may go through the whole week-end without saying a word, just sitting in a corner and *thinking* or walking in the garden. I felt I ought just to tell you this. It doesn't mean she's not enjoying herself. She's just shy.'

Faced with the prospect of one either silent or disapproving guest, we awaited the coming of the Nicolsons with some anxiety. They were to come separately as Harold was giving a lecture at All Souls and Vita was coming directly from London. At approximately the appointed hour of their arrival it began to rain and continued to do so with increasing intensity. We waited. No guests arrived. We waited longer and at last the front door bell rang. In those dear dead days we had a parlourmaid but so great was our nervous state that, as one, we sprang to open the front door.

There on the doorstep stood a drenched and bedraggled figure who had apparently arrived on foot. Eccentric though we knew Vita to be, we could not believe that she had *walked* from London (or perhaps even Sissinghurst) to Garsington. She was, however, clearly in distress, wet through and with all the incipient symptoms of a bad cold. We hailed her in and she proceeded to drip silently in the front hall. At last she braced herself to explain. She had run out of petrol somewhere just outside Garsington and had indeed walked to our door in the downpour, thinking, quite correctly, that this was more sensible than searching for a petrol pump in an unknown village. Having got this straight, she suffered herself to be borne off by Ruth for ministration and comfort.

At that moment the rain stopped and the sun appeared, and I started off in search of the abandoned car. By the time I had found and refuelled it and returned with it to our house, Harold had arrived from Oxford and was waiting, lonely and disconsolate as any Peri, on the loggia.

Despite this inauspicious opening, our week-end was a great success. No one could have been less shy than Vita, or more genuinely admiring of our garden, despite its display of zinnias (which she declared she had never seen before,' antirrhinums (which she contentedly called 'snap dragons') and 'morning glory', which she also failed to recognise. Ruth's morale was greatly heightened, Vita was relaxed and talkative and amusing, and Harold sat in the manner of an agreeably surprised nanny whose usually difficult charge is behaving impeccably.

But the great occasion of the week-end was, of course, the publication of Harold's life of King George V. It had actually appeared on the Thursday before to a chorus of acclaim, which swelled to a paean of unalloyed praise from the *Sunday Times* and the *Observer*. Harold was most justifiably elated and read and re-read the encomiums with immense pleasure. He had sent me a copy of the book, which he most charmingly inscribed, and while he devoted himself to his own pleasure, I was engrossed in the cause of the praise in which he was delighting.

And how eminently warranted were the tributes. Apart from its elegance of style, its depth of understanding of character and personality and the degree of its scholarship, Harold's biography of King George V is a model of its kind and an example to all who labour in that field. It has also been recognised as a standard work on the tangled constitutional issues of the period. It is in every way a triumph of authorship, knowledge and readability.

I am not, I think, a man of unusually precipitate reactions but as I read Harold's splendid book for the first time I felt my imagination kindled by a desire for emulation. I have always been a staunch, and perhaps even a romantic, monarchist and such expertise as I had lay in the field of contemporary history. The prospect of writing the life of one's sovereign and combining this with the narrative of one's own times and illustrating the role and responsibility of the monarch in these great events held for me at that moment the highest ambition in life, and I was prompted to say something of the sort to Harold Nicolson as we sat together on the sunlit loggia. I congratulated him warmly and sincerely on his masterpiece, and then I added, 'I can't think of anything more fascinating than to do for George VI what you've done for his father. I'd give anything to do it.' '*Would* you?' he replied, and returned to immerse himself anew in the roseate flood of eulogium.

It was, I recall, a happy week-end. Ruth and I had a luncheon-party at which Vita was completely charming, and the Nicolsons left on Monday morning without our mentioning again the subject on which I had touched so impetuously. I had plenty, however, to occupy my mind. I was putting the finishing touches to *The Nemesis of Power* and was still a regular attendant at the Foreign Office in one capacity or another. Months passed without my thinking again of the vision which had opened suddenly before my eyes on that August morning at Garsington. I had indeed completely forgotten it until, in November of that year, it was brought up again abruptly by the receipt of a letter, courteous yet titillating my curiosity, inviting me to call upon the Queen's Private Secretary at Buckingham Palace.

I did not know Sir Alan Lascelles well; indeed I had only met him, apart from casual encounters in Brooks's, once before when – as I have recounted in an earlier chapter – with Moley Sargent I had gone to consult him on a delicate matter connected with the captured German documents. Now I found him alone in his office, a room with which, together with himself and his two successors, I was destined to become intimately familiar over the next twenty-five years.

Tommy Lascelles is cast in the same mould as Moley Sargent, indeed they were not dissimilar even in appearance. Tall and aristocratic of bearing, with a long face and long thin hands and feet, his manner was at the outset austere, but I soon came to discover that behind this lay a wry and somewhat sardonic sense of humour and an immense degree of kindness. His background had been varied: educated at Marlborough and Christ Church, he had been soldier, aide-de-camp and son-in-law to a Viceroy of India, a stockbroker and courtier, and now occupied one of the most important and most anonymous offices in the state, that of principal private secretary to the sovereign. I came to know and appreciate and respect his shrewd judgement, the delightful and unusual workings of his mind, his courage and common-sense in time of crisis and his essentially sound sense of values. He had played a vital part in the great events which he had witnessed at close quarters and his wisdom had on many occasions pointed the way to wise decisions. From this encounter on 24 November 1952 there developed a warm friendship which I am happy to say still obtains, though Tommy is now pushing 90, and in the course of my future task it was to his friendly guidance and encouragement I was to owe perhaps more than to anything else. No critic could be more wise, more trenchant or more constructive.

But at our first interview this intimacy had not yet developed. He was courteous and I was respectful, and though I was consumed with curiosity, hope and some temerity, he subsequently assured me that I was outwardly calm!

Tommy came straight to the point. 'Your name has been suggested to me as a suitable biographer for King George VI.' (Some time later I learned that the suggestion had come from Harold Nicolson, who had been less self-centred on that summer morning than I had suspected!) 'I have read your life of Hindenburg,' Tommy Lascelles continued, 'and others of your works. They are excellent – and I may say I have also checked on your character. Now supposing I put this proposal to you as a hypothetical proposition, what would your answer be?'

'My hypothetical answer?' I asked, with as innocent a face as I could muster.

'Your hypothetical answer, of course,' he answered with the ghost of a smile.

'Hypothetically speaking, then, my answer would be a resounding "yes",' I replied.

'Thank you, that's all I wanted to know,' said Tommy. 'Good morning. You will, of course, treat this matter in the strictest confidence until you hear further from me.'

I left the Palace in a state of some bewilderment. It would be unwise to build too great hopes upon so 'hypothetical' a proposition, but yet I had a persistent feeling in my bones that the job would be mine. This did not, however, allay my basic anxiety and uncertainty, and my pledge of secrecy precluded me from any discussion of the matter save with Ruth. I must confess that I passed the next days in a state of nervous misgiving, and then there came a further gleam from the dark lantern at the Palace. A message from Tommy Lascelles informed me that Her Majesty Queen Elizabeth the Queen Mother would receive me on 17 December.

It was with some trepidation that I walked across Green Park from the Ritz to Buckingham Palace that morning. I had not met 'the Royals', save most formally at levées, garden-parties, investitures and the like, and the thought of a *tête-à-tête* with the Queen Mother was awesome to me. I felt an unwonted diffidence unnerving me, and then suddenly I decided that the only possible way to behave under these circumstances was to be perfectly natural and at once shyness left me and confidence returned.

Had I been a prey to the most abject bashfulness, it would have been instantly dissipated by the gracious kindness of my reception. Queen Elizabeth, beautiful in her mourning, greeted me with a warmth and charm which I have never forgotten and which has remained unvarying throughout the succeeding years during which she has been so wonderful a friend to Ruth and me.

On this first day of our meeting I realised that we were still in the hypothetical stage. Her Majesty had evidently received a favourable report from Tommy Lascelles but wished to see for herself what manner of man I was. (She has since told me that she had expected to see an elderly professor with a long white beard!) I could feel that she was appraising me and hoped with all my heart that I was passing the test. The Queen Mother repeated Tommy's questions as to what my answer would be to a hypothetical proposition that I should write the King's life, and I replied in rather lengthier terms than I had to Tommy. I could conceive of no greater honour and no more happy a task and I indicated that, should it become my welcome lot to undertake this, I should hope to be granted much help from her. She gave me that dazzling smile which gave away nothing and a short while later the audience ended.

I lunched that day with Tommy and Joan Lascelles in their delightful apartments in St James's Palace which had once been Fanny Burney's, and he asked for an account of the interview. At the end of my recital he made no comment but again enjoined secrecy upon me.

So, apart from the pleasure of a delightful audience, I was still in limbo and remained there until after Ruth had sailed for Virginia on 31 December on her annual visit to her mother. I was thus deprived of my sole confidant and the suspense was becoming unbearable until, on the morning of Saturday, 10 January, the local Garsington exchange was thrown into a state of confusion by a person-to-person call for me from Sandringham. I was cutting wood at the time at the far end of the property and it took me some time to reach the telephone. The dry, sardonic voice of Tommy Lascelles asked me in a matter of fact tone, 'The Queen wants to know how you're geting on?'

'With what?' I asked with, I think, pardonable uncertainty.

'With the life of her father, of course,' was Tommy's disconcerting reply.

'But Tommy,' I stammered, 'it's still in a "hypothetical" stage, and I'm not allowed to discuss it with anyone. If it's a real offer, oughtn't I to have something in writing? And shouldn't there be an announcement?'

'I suppose you are right,' said Tommy. 'Both the Queen and her mother are delighted that you will undertake the job. We had better discuss details together. Could you come and see me on Monday morning at the Palace?'

I said that I could and would. As a result of our conference I received a written warrant as a royal biographer and that afternoon I signed a contract with Macmillan. The official announcement appeared in *The Times* and in the press generally on 9 February.

Royal biography is virtually as old as monarchy itself. The tablets of Babylon, the papyri of Egypt and large portions of the Old Testament were among our progenitors; Plutarch, Suetonius, Voltaire and Carlyle, even Shakespeare and Marlowe were of our number. Indeed if the latest campaign to rehabilitate King Richard III should prove successful, the Bard of Avon may stand indicted as being a participant in one of the greatest smear campaigns in history.

It is, however, only within the last 125 years that this important aspect of history has been officially recognised and categorised. There is, of course, nothing in the world to prevent anyone from becoming the biographer of any monarch in any country. But if he should desire the co-operation of officialdom in writing of the British royal family he must come within one of two classifications: he must be either 'approved' or 'official'.

An approved biographer is one who, of his own volition, conceives a desire to write the life of some sovereign or other member of the royal family and, if his status be confirmed as that of an established and genuinely bona fide scholar and the Sovereign's permission has been granted, he will receive invaluable, generous, and courteous assistance from the staff of the Royal Archives at Windsor, who will accord him free access to their treasures. With this aid such writers as Elizabeth Longford and Cecil Woodham-Smith have produced their admirable studies of Queen Victoria, Philip Magnus of King Edward VII, and Georgina Battiscombe of Queen Alexandra. All such works are subject to submission to the Sovereign through the Keeper of the Royal Archives or his deputy, the Royal Librarian. In a class by herself, however, is Frances Donaldson, who has recently achieved her own particular triumph in producing her life of King Edward VIII without benefit of official documentation at all.

An official royal biographer is different. He is formally appointed by the Sovereign on the counsel of his or her personal advisers. Whoever is thus appointed has been previously screened and vetted as to discretion and security, and is therefore adjudged meet for unrestricted access to the Royal Archives and to government papers contained therein, and his use of them is left to his own judgement and prudence. If he is wise he maintains the closest liaison with the Sovereign's Private Secretary and the Royal Librarian, and with the Secretary to the Cabinet, but his ultimate censors are the Sovereign personally and the relict of the subject of the biography.

These 'ground rules' were not promulgated in canon form. They simply developed with experience, beginning some hundred years ago when Queen Victoria appointed Theodore Martin to be the official biographer of the Prince Consort. It had originally been intended that the Prince's life should be written by his former Private Secretary, General Charles Grey, who on the death of his master had assumed a similar office with the Queen – in fact but not in name, since the post of Private Secretary was not established until 1867. He had indeed completed an introductory volume entitled *The Early Years of the Prince Consort* which was published in 1868, but had discovered that the demands and burdens of his official duties precluded his continuing further with this great task. He therefore recommended to the Queen a man of good scholastic background, fifty years of age.

Theodore Martin did not accept the task instantly and unconditionally. With the integrity of a biographer he stipulated that he should have a free hand as to the time and manner in which the work should be carried out and to this the Queen agreed. She did not, however, allow him unfettered access to her own papers and those of the Prince Consort, and it is recorded that she 'personally undertook the sifting of the documents which were to be placed at Mr Martin's disposal'. It is also known that she exercised an indefatigable interest in the enterprise.

Despite, or perhaps because of, this royal collaboration,

Martin completed his monumental five-volume work in as many years. His first tome appeared in 1875, his fifth in 1880 and – for the nostalgic delectation of modern publishers and the general reading public alike – a cheap edition (six parts at 6d. each) was issued a year later.

During the execution of this arduous task the biographer was refreshed by sustaining drafts from the Fount of Honour. In 1878 the Queen bestowed on him a C.B. – the lemon at half-time as it were – and raised him to K.C.B. at the conclusion of his work. She appointed him a K.C.V.O. in 1896.

Sir Martin's task could not have been an easy one, however, with The Widow of Windsor breathing down his neck, as it were. It must be recorded to his credit that, though his view of Prince Albert was highly favourable, its tone was essentially candid and free from courtly adulation. Queen Victoria was greatly pleased with the result and bestowed inscribed copies upon her many relations with the same prodigality that she presented busts of Prince Albert. I remember that when I visited the Kaiser at Doorn in August 1939 (as described in *Knaves, Fools and Heroes*), I found his set of Sir Theodore Martin's volumes in a remarkably pristine condition.

There does not exist an official life of Queen Victoria. No single reason for this omission is to be found. Her great age at her death would have made it difficult for a biographer writing in 1902 to recapture with accuracy the atmosphere and personal climate of ideas prevailing in her early youth and the beginning of her reign. But the need for authentic information on the Queen's activities was felt at the outset of the new reign, and gave rise to a ten-volume series entitled *Letters of Queen Victoria*, which, though not a biography, was 'official' in the sense that editors were picked for the task and given free access to her papers.

The writing of the life of King Edward VII arose from a highly complicated series of events, too complex, indeed, to be dealt with here in detail. Suffice it to say that in

February 1914, after lengthy discussions, the consent of the Sovereign was given for the authorisation of Sir Sidney Lee, then editor of *The Dictionary of National Biography*, to write a short biography of the late King with emphasis on the period of his reign. Before, however, he could begin his researches the First World War intervened and nothing was done. After the war the project was resumed, and expanded to a two-volume biography, the first to cover the period before the accession, and the second the reign.

Lee was not given unreserved access to the Royal Archives, which had been officially established in 1911. At first he was shown only papers looked out for him by Sir Frederick Ponsonby, but when the biography entered its second volume phase he was allowed to work in the Archives to a limited extent.

The first of Lee's volumes appeared in 1925, but he died in the following year before he could complete the second. This was eventually compiled from his notes by his assistant, F. S. Markham, and was published in 1927. It was a work of scholarly distinction.

On the suggestion of King George VI's advisers, the novel decision was taken that the life of King George V should be in a dichotomised form. To Mr John Gore fell the task of writing the *private* life, while, after the Second World War, Harold Nicolson was entrusted with the *public* life of the sovereign. John Gore's admirable and important work appeared in 1941, and eleven years later Harold produced what is one of the outstanding biographical and historical studies of our time. He received the K.C.V.O. in 1953.

The last official biographer to be appointed was James Pope-Hennessy, whose tragic and brutal murder deprived the world of letters of one of its most gifted denizens. To him was confided the writing of the life of Queen Mary, and there came from his pen a most delightful and entertaining volume. Incidentally, Queen Mary is the only royal consort since Prince Albert to be accorded an official biography.

The dichotomised form of biography did not prove a success. It is impossible to separate the private from the official life of any public character, let alone that of a sovereign, and though John Gore's book was excellent in itself, Harold Nicolson had perforce to cover much of the same ground to give a full-length portrait of his subject in its proper perspective.

A lesson had been learned, and when I was appointed it was made perfectly clear to me that I was to deal with all aspects of the life of King George VI, although I gladly concurred in Tommy Lascelles's subsequent suggestion that the King as a sportsman and countryman should be the subject of a special study by Aubrey Buxton, who had been a friend and neighbour in Norfolk and shared for many years King George's delight in dog-and-gun.

Like Sidney Lee and Harold Nicolson, I was given an absolutely free hand – nothing, so far as I know, was ever withheld from me of either a public or a private nature. The King's letters and diaries were placed unreservedly at my disposal and it was made known by the Queen that all who had had association with her father in any capacity should make me free of their correspondence with him and share their recollections, whatever their nature might be, with me. No biographer could have been more completely trusted or facilitated than I was, and I felt deeply honoured by this confidence.

As had been, and remains, my technique of writing history and biography, I pursued the triple formula of reading the published works of the period, consulting the documents and talking with as many persons as possible who had known the King. These last varied from Queen Mary, by whom I was fortunate enough to be received three times before her death just prior to the coronation, and who gave

F

me a poignant account of the Duke of York's agony of mind during the crisis of the abdication, to the aged pensioner who had been nursery footman at York Cottage, Sandringham, and who delivered himself of the immortal line, 'Many a royal fore'ead this 'and has 'eld, sir.'

From the Duke of Windsor I learned of the early life of the princes at York Cottage, and of the diabolical schemes which they would concoct to torment their pompous tutor, Mr Hassell. I saw him both in London and in Paris and he was extremely helpful on this early period, though I found the Duchess less interested in this aspect of his life and more anxious to discuss the time-worn grievances of the abdication.

I was the guest of the Queen and of the Queen Mother at Windsor, Balmoral, Sandringham, Birkhall and Royal Lodge, and gained thereby an invaluable appreciation of the King's pattern of life. Prince Philip and Princess Margaret talked to me of their very different relationships with their respective father-in-law and father. Kindness, co-operation and enjoyment were everywhere.

An early problem to be faced was where I should work. During his years of authorship on George V I had listened to Harold Nicolson's incessant grumblings about the conditions at Windsor. He had a positive threnody of complaints. The Round Tower (in which the Royal Archives are housed) was so cold that he had to take a rug and wear mittens. As there were no catering facilities he had to take sandwiches from home – though what prevented him from walking down the hill and lunching comfortably at the White Hart I could never understand. Finally the train service from Paddington to Windsor was appalling, often entailing a change at Slough. Had I ever been to Slough? There was no need to pause for thought before answering: if I had been there I could never under any circumstances have forgotten such a horrible experience. How thankful he was when, his researches completed, he could retire to the comforts of Sissinghurst to write his book.

Even allowing for Harold's gift for humorous exaggeration, not to mention the streak of enjoyable martyrdom which was one of his salient characteristics, I was, in fact, somewhat daunted by his Grimm's fairy-tale description of his sufferings. I asked Tommy Lascelles where the files of the last reign were, and on finding they were still in Buckingham Palace I made a plea that they might be kept there for the time being and that some corner might be found for me and my secretary to work in their vicinity. Tommy was frankly doubtful. He explained that although Buckingham Palace looked very large, there was very little spare space in it. I suggested the abandoned air-raid shelter which loomed outside the window of his own office, but this apparently had been given over to storage, and we parted with some murmur on his part of perhaps a garret somewhere in St James's Palace, a prospect which, though not exactly rosy, still seemed preferable to Harold Nicolson's dolours.

In the end the problem of housing me was solved by the Queen herself and under somewhat singular circumstances. It so happened that I had received a C.M.G. in the Coronation Honours and in due course I was summoned to an investiture to receive my decoration from the Queen. These occasions are deeply impressive and, though lacking the panoply of the days when full parade uniform was worn *de rigueur*, they are still brilliant and lustrous. They are also timed to run to a split second by the Lord Chamberlain's Office and that great functionary himself keeps an eagle eye on every detail.

Because in those days a double-barrelled patronymic was alphabetised under the last name, I was marshalled under the Bs and hence fairly early among the recipients. We had been warned not to linger ('loiter' I think was the word used by Lord Scarbrough, the Lord Chamberlain) and I was therefore not a little surprised when the Queen engaged me in conversation. She had been thinking, she said, about where best I could work on her father's life, and had decided that it would be best if I could do it in Buckingham Palace 'where the security was good and I could leave things lying about'. Would I like to work in the Pine Room, which was big enough to hold both me and my secretary and convenient to the Private Secretary's office which was just below it? Overwhelmed by surprise and gratitude at such kindness and consideration, and delighted at having my problem thus happily solved, I was yet conscious of a certain congestion of traffic building up behind me and of an irate Roger Scarbrough enpurpled and, metaphorically speaking, stop-watch in hand. I, however, was enjoying myself, and at any rate I could do nothing about it until Her Majesty released me. So we settled it all very comfortably and arranged that I should work out the details with Tommy Lascelles. I expressed my heartfelt thanks for Her Majesty's gracious thoughtfulness and, having run the gauntlet of Roger Scarbrough's wrath, I rejoined Ruth and my sister Irene in the body of the Throne Room, there to be reproved again for holding up the proceedings. It did take a little explaining.

For the next four years I worked on research and the gathering of information, with the Pine Room as my headquarters and with the assistance of my much loved and highly efficient niece and secretary, Juliet Heaton, who only deserted me for the higher calls of matrimony when, in 1956, she married Oliver Fiennes, now Dean of Lincoln. She was succeeded by Frances Coulson who remained my devoted assistant for the next eighteen years. A vast quantity of material passed over my desk, and I talked with more than 200 people, exclusive of members of the Royal Family. I travelled widely, visiting the length and breadth of England and also foreign countries with which, or with whose rulers and statesmen, King George had been associated. These included the United States, Canada, France, the Netherlands,

Norway. I also talked with the King's ministers in this country and learned from them many things. Mr Churchill, for example, told me how in 1940 he had overcome the King's disappointment at not having Lord Halifax as Prime Minister instead of himself. From an initial reserve, he said, there had developed 'a degree of intimacy which had never existed between sovereign and prime minister since the days of my ancestor and Queen Anne', and described how at their famous Tuesday luncheon audiences they would help one another from a serving trolley: 'For I could not allow my Sovereign to give me meat and potatoes without performing the same office for him.'

Mr Attlee, too, described the conditions after the war under which he willingly surrendered to King George the unfettered freedom of bestowing the Orders of the Garter and the Thistle, which had, since the days of George I and Robert Walpole, been granted by the Sovereign only 'on the advice of ministers'.

Clem Attlee was far from being the clam he was often alleged to be. I became very fond of him, and when he became a neighbour of ours after his retirement he often visited us at Garsington, where he would talk 'a blue streak'. If he trusted you he would drop his reserve and I discovered that he was at heart a romantic. His brother was that Father Attlee who while at Oxford had become the Secretary of the White Rose League dedicated to the preservation of the memory of King Charles the Martyr, and Mr Attlee himself was a devotee of Anthony Hope. I once asked him how he came to hit upon the inspired choice of Lord Mountbatten as Viceroy of India and was delighted with his reply: 'Rather a Ruritanian figure, don't you think?' I at once had a vision of Dickie Mountbatten sporting the Order of the Red Rose!

He also told me of his lifelong regret at having prevented Ramsay MacDonald, whose P.P.S. he had been but whom he never forgave for betraying the Labour Party in 1931, from attending his first Buckingham Palace garden party as

Prime Minister in morning dress and a bowler hat. 'One should never yield to better instincts,' was his comment.

I remember very well taking a copy of his book *As It Happened* with me to the House of Commons and asking him to inscribe it for me. He did so and as he wrote he looked up over his spectacles. 'It's a pedestrian little work, isn't it?' he asked with endearing candour. And of course it was.

I recall that Lord Attlee also regaled me on several occasions with recitations of doggerel of his own composition reflecting – not always too kindly – on his Party colleagues. It has always been my fervent hope that these gems were committed to paper and that their author's biographer will bring them to light.

Of all King George's Commonwealth Ministers with whom I talked, perhaps the most impressive was Eamon de Valera, the only one of them whom the King never met, and one who had not scrupled to shed both British and Irish blood to achieve the independence of his country. When 'Dev' came to London in 1937, to negotiate with Mr Chamberlain the return to Eire of the Irish ports over which Britain had retained rights under the Anglo-Irish Treaty of 1921, some hope had been entertained of his being received in audience by the King, who welcomed the chance of meeting this former rebel against the Crown, but in the end this was judged to be inopportune and no subsequently propitious moment for such a meeting ever occurred.

This was brought home to me when I first met Mr de Valera, when he was leader of the opposition in the Dail. He asked me why I had come to see him and I explained that I was writing the life of King George VI and wished to talk with as many as possible of those who had served him in high office. 'But why me?' Dev asked. 'For I never saw your King.' 'No, but you were his last Irish Prime Minister,' I answered. 'I was *what?*' came the amazed reply.

'I do not recognise myself in that part.' 'I know you took the oath of allegiance in order to be able to abolish it,' I replied, 'but you did take it and therefore you were his last Irish Prime Minister.'

At first I thought that the long saturine face was to be convulsed with fury and the fierce sightless eyes would blaze in anger, but what I took for anger proved to be humour and he laughed aloud. From that moment there arose what I like to think was a degree of friendship, for I saw him not infrequently later, both when he was Taoiseach and later as President of the Republic. As he grew to trust me he talked of events in modern Irish history which fascinated me, for it has long been one of my special subjects. But first he had his little joke with me.

'Why do you come to Ireland so much?' he once asked me. 'Do you really like it?'

'Indeed I do,' I answered, 'but I can't think why, for you twice tried to assassinate my father.'

'And when was that?' he asked with interest.

'In the Fenian troubles,' I said, and went on to tell him that in the course of one ambush, papa had his top hat shot off his head. 'Ah, they took their politics seriously in those days!' was Dev's reply.

I asked him why he had not come himself again in December 1921 to negotiate the treaty with Lloyd George, with whom he had established a good rapport during the preliminary talks on the truce in the summer of that year. 'What, and leave all my cabinet behind me? I shouldn't have lasted five minutes,' was his reply, but he went on to denounce Lloyd George and Winston Churchill for their guile and subtlety in seducing Arthur Griffith and Michael Collins from their loyalty to the principle of a republican goverment in Ireland to accepting the compromise of 'dominion status'. This Dev never forgave and he also never ceased to inveigh against the partition of Ulster from the rest of Eire.

I also put it to him whether he would ever have severed

the silver cord of the External Relations Act, which bound the Republic of Ireland to the British Crown by acknowledging the right of the sovereign to issue the credentials of Eire's diplomatic representatives in foreign countries. This piece of vital legislation, which had been the basic foundation of de Valera's association with the Commonwealth, had been repealed by John Costello's government in 1949, when Dev had been in opposition. He said emphatically that he would never have done so, and I remarked how ironic it was that Eire should have severed its links with the Crown at the very moment that the Commonwealth countries, by the formula of April 1949, had agreed that their membership might include republican forms of government who yet recognised the British sovereign as head of the Commonwealth. He agreed, but 'jibbed' and 'put his ears back', as it were, when I described him as the artificer of the new British Commonwealth – which in effect he was.

But there was a greatness about Dev which was undeniable, and I like to recall those hours I spent with him in his sunny room at what had been Viceregal Lodge but was now the Presidential Residence. He would sit like an old blind eagle, though his eyes still pierced one's soul. I would listen to him say, with a wintry smile, in answer to my question whether he had ever put down any biographical notes on paper, that the only occasions he had time to think about that was when he was 'on the run', or I would hear all the sadness and tragedy of Ireland in his voice as he spoke of some dead revolutionary comrade, for example Padraic Pearse.

Characteristically, at the end of his second Presidential term of office in 1973, de Valera retired to the modest seclusion of a convalescent home in Blackrock, near Dublin. There he died, at the splendid age of 92, on 30 August 1975.

In the course of my researches, both written and oral, I found that, like his father and grandfather before him, King

George VI was keenly aware of his loyalties and obligations as a member of the Guild of Sovereigns, which he regarded in the sense of a royal trade union. Being himself so conscious of his own responsibilities he was ever sympathetic with the burdens and difficulties of his fellow monarchs. It was in a great measure this guild-loyalty – over and above the ties of kinship and the bonds of common humanity – which prompted the warmth and hospitality with which he received King Haakon of Norway, Queen Wilhelmina of the Netherlands and King George of Greece during their temporary wartime exile; which induced the sympathy he displayed with King Peter of Yugoslavia and King Michael of Rumania in the circumstances which rendered their exile more permanent; and which evoked his broad-minded understanding of the terrible dilemmas which beset King Leopold of the Belgians, Prince Paul of Yugoslavia and King Boris of Bulgaria. 'Mon métier est à moi d'être roi,' King Edward VII had said on a memorable occasion, and this was also the attitude of his grandson, who could not be indifferent to the fortunes and misfortunes of his fellow guildsmen.

I was fortunate enough to be received in audience by a number of these monarchs and in the course of our conversations I made two discoveries. The first was the unanimous respect, admiration and almost reverence which they entertained for King George, not only because of his generous hospitality but also because of his natural leadership among the heads of states who had become the victims of Nazi aggression. Not only had he given them asylum but by his example and his simple faith he had sustained them in their adversity and given them hope for the future. As King Michael of Rumania said of him to me, 'King George gave me advice which I have always tried to follow both as a king and a man.'

The second fact which was brought home to me with great poignancy was the soul-searing, traumatic choice presented to all heads of state in the event of the total occupation of their countries by an enemy aggressor. This decision is one of hideous complexity and it inevitably arrives when there is little time for calm consideration. To leave their homeland and follow their governments into exile leaves them open to the charge of desertion by those who remain behind; yet to remain involves the risk of their being held hostage for the submissive conduct of their peoples held in the thraldom of a ruthless conqueror. During the Second World War this onerous alternative was forced upon Queen Wilhelmina of the Netherlands, King Haakon of Norway, King Christian of Denmark and King Leopold of the Belgians. Two chose exile and the gallant continuation of the struggle from a foreign shore against a common enemy with the justified hope of ultimate victory and liberation. Of the two who remained in their respective countries, King Christain, by his daily ride through the streets of his capital and his gallant championship of his Jewish subjects, became the symbol of resistance by the Danish people to a fate which they had been powerless to prevent but to which they were determined not to be resigned. But the decision of King Leopold to remain was one of the darkest personal tragedies of the war, and one in which King George took a deep and sympathetic interest.

Yet whatever the decision taken, each monarch found criticism in his or her country when the great day of liberation had dawned and waned, and the post-war problems became immediate. As Queen Wilhelmina so wisely remarked, 'Whatever we did we could not please everybody.'

I treasure the memory of my association with these sovereigns because of their kindness, simplicity, courtesy and their obvious desire to be helpful. I cannot recall a single instance in which I was not put at my ease immediately, and I frequently found the most fascinating anecdotes and reminiscences arising in our conversations, some relevant, some irrelevant, some unexpected.

For example, I was surprised to find that in talking with

King Haakon in the Royal Palace at Oslo the name of Vidkun Quisling obtruded itself, and His Majesty was both amazed and interested to learn that I had unknowingly encountered the Norwegian traitor, whose name has now passed into the language of infamy, during a visit to Moscow in 1929.

It was King Haakon who told me one of the best stories about King George. After the harrowing experiences which both he and Queen Wilhelmina had gone through at the hands of Nazi commando bands bent upon their capture, they agreed that as refugee monarchs in London they should impress upon their hosts the risks and dangers of such attacks. It was decided that King Haakon should take this initiative, and he chose an occasion to ask King George what would happen in the event of a parachute attack on Buckingham Palace. King George explained the method of alerting the guard, but King Haakon, somewhat sceptically, asked to see it in operation. Obligingly, King George pressed the alarm signal and, together with the Queen, they all went into the garden to watch the result. 'What happened, Sir?' I asked, for King Haakon had paused at this point of his story. 'Exactly nothing happened,' was his reply.

It appeared that complete anti-climax had indeed prevailed. An anxious equerry dispatched to make inquiries had returned with the report that the officer of the guard had been informed by the police-sergeant on duty that no attack was impending 'as he had heard nothing about it'. Police co-operation having been obtained, a number of guardsmen entered the gardens at the double and proceeded to thrash the undergrowth in the manner of beaters at a shoot rather than of men engaged in the pursuit of a dangerous enemy. 'I was appalled,' said King Haakon to me, 'but your King and Queen just roared with laughter.' For the record, be it said that as a result of this incident precautions were revised and strengthened.

It was at Claridges that, with some emotion, King Peter, the last prince of the House of Karageorgevic to occupy the Yugoslav throne, told me of the not inconsiderable assistance given him by King George in the complicated arrangement of his marriage. He also confirmed to me the story of the saving of his life by King George – then Duke of York – on the occasion of his baptism, at which the Duke was *Koom* (godfather). Belgrade Cathedral was cold, the naked child had been borne by the reluctant Duke on a velvet cushion and placed in the trembling, icy hands of the Patriarch of Serbia, who promptly dropped him into the font. With the traditional initiative of a naval officer, the Duke scooped up the gulping child and restored him to safe custody. 'Though I suppose I may be called an eyewitness of this event,' King Peter said with a twinkle, 'I can't lay claim to any clear recollection of it, but I can assure you that I have been told this story all my life as an accepted truth.' Later, with tears in his eyes, he told me the tragic story of his father's assassination at Marseilles in October 1934, and of which I have written in *Knaves, Fools and Heroes*. King Peter attributed his father's, King Alexander's, death to the fact that, for a variety of mischances, he had not worn his steel-mesh bullet-proof shirt.

In a villa on the shores of Lake Geneva I was received by King Michael of Rumania and his charming consort, Queen Anne-Marie. Here, as I have said, I found one of King George's most fervent admirers and I developed a considerable respect for this young monarch, who, in his brief life and reign, had suffered many and diverse adversities. Called to the throne in September 1940 at the age of nineteen, after the abdication of his father King Carol II at the behest of the pro-Nazi dictator, Marshal Ion Antonescu, Michael was caught up in a whirlwind of events which it was beyond his ability to control. By the end of October there were eighteen German divisions in Rumania and the country was completely under the control of the Reich. On 23 November, Antonescu formally adhered to the Tripartite Pact in Berlin and, in company with his Axis allies, declared war on the Soviet Union in June 1941. King Michael had little say in these proceedings and no sympathy for the policies which they represented. He had inherited the pro-British proclivities of his father and was bitterly antagonistic to the views of Antonescu. It was his ambition to encompass the fall of the dictator and bring Rumania into the Western camp. But he was young and immature and he had to bide his time. One does not bring down a dictator, even in Rumania, with a puff of wind. It was three years before the opportunity occurred, largely as a result of the cruel losses sustained by the Rumanian troops in casualties and prisoners at Stalingrad, and even then the King was desperately uncertain as to whom he could trust implicitly in such a venture.

As he told me the story over the tea tray in the warm drawing-room of a Swiss villa, I was impressed by his restraint, his lack of emotion and his remarkable modesty. For it was the King himself who master-minded the coup of 23 August 1944, himself holding Antonescu covered while the gentlemen of his household disarmed the Marshal's aides, and who, holding them prisoner, had declared war on the Axis Powers. Though his action came too late to save Rumania and her ruling house from the substitution of a Soviet for a Nazi tyranny, there are not many monarchs in modern times, outside Ruritania, who have taken so direct and formidable a part in the affairs of their country.

Certainly the most impressive of this royal galaxy was Queen Wilhelmina, who received me after her abdication and as Princess of the Netherlands. She had been the longest reigning monarch in Europe, having succeeded as a minor in 1890 and vacating the throne in favour of her daughter Princess Juliana in 1948. In the course of her long reign she had seen much, suffered much and weathered many complex situations, constitutional and international, in the handling of which she had displayed outstanding wisdom, courage and determination.

Queen Wilhelmina, as I must continue to call her, was indubitably an awesome personality, and I remember that when I was on a visit to The Hague shortly before the war, the Prime Minister, Hendrikus Colijn, a tough old officer of the colonial army turned politician, had spoken of the formidable presence which she exercised during the cabinet meetings over which she presided. In certain respects she resembled Queen Victoria, who, in her moments of displeasure, could make such aristocrats as Lord Salisbury quake and Prince Bismarck sweat.

Nothing, however, could have been more kind and gracious than her reception of me – once it was arranged. The British embassy having completely failed in this respect, the whole business was set in motion smoothly and efficiently by my old friend and wartime comrade, Tommy Stone, of whom I have written in *Knaves, Fools and Heroes*, who was then Canadian Ambassador to the Netherlands, and with whom Ruth and I were staying.

On her abdication Queen Wilhelmina had retired to the royal residence of Het Loo, built by Prince William of Orange before he became King William III as a hunting lodge of simple beauty in an architectural design of black and white. It was set in a great beech wood, the hub of a wheel of which the spokes were a pattern of rides and avenues. Vernal vistas stretched into the green shadows and, on the hot shimmering day on which I went there, the whole place had the air of an enchanted palace in a fairy forest. Moreover, it seemed to be deserted save for an aged retainer and a single veteran courtier who conducted me into a garden room filled with chintz-covered furniture.

Queen Wilhelmina, though of medium stature and Victorian build, had great and majestic dignity. She was also most kind and hospitable and regaled me with china tea, sandwiches and chocolate cake. Once we had got into the swing of conversation she talked frankly and, at times, humorously, and gave me information invaluable to the biographer. She confirmed exactly, for example, the account which I had found in King George's diary of their historic telephone conversation of 13 May 1940, when she had appealed as sovereign to sovereign for more aircraft to be sent for the defence of Holland. Alas, there was little the King could do but pass on her appeal to the persons directly concerned, but this did not deter this intrepid royal lady from making a dash across the North Sea in a destroyer to Harwich to repeat her agonised request.

'Did you not consider going on to London, Ma'am?' I asked, and was a little disconcerted by her reply. 'No, why should I? There is a very good hotel in Harwich.'

My curiosity overcame me to the degree of asking her what costume she had worn on this memorable and sudden departure, and I was delighted with her almost coy response. 'Oh, just a little two-piece suit and a *very* old hat.' The hat was shortly abandoned for a steel helmet on board the destroyer.

We talked of other matters and I told her of my genuine admiration for the adamant courage which she had displayed on several historic occasions. For example, she had permitted President Paul Kruger to reside within her borders after his flight from the Transvaal despite the expressed disapproval of the British Government. Again, she had insisted on the disarmament of the German troops as a condition of their passage through the Dutch province of Limburg during their retreat in October 1918; and again she had fearlessly confronted and outfaced the revolutionary movement of Pieter Troelstra in her own capital that same winter. And, most intrepid of all, she had calmly and successfully defied the threats and menaces of the Allied and Associated Powers in 1920 in refusing to surrender to them for trial as a war criminal the person of Kaiser Wilhelm II, to whom she had granted asylum two years earlier at the conclusion of the war.

The Queen spoke on all these subjects with the calm view

of history, giving her reasons for her several actions with an almost academic detachment, deploying the pros and cons with remarkable lack of reserve. She was conscious of the important role which she had played in world events and was assured, as it seemed to me rightly, of her outstanding place not only in the history of her own country but of Europe.

We parted in the spirit of Mr Disraeli's 'We authors, Ma'am.' I promised to send Her Majesty my *Nemesis of Power*, which had recently appeared, and she responded shortly thereafter with a copy of her memoirs, *Lonely But Not Alone*, with a charming inscription. I left her presence knowing that I had been privileged to talk with a great sovereign and a great lady.

Anglo-American relations had played a large part in the political thinking of King George VI and the personal friendship which was engendered between himself and President Roosevelt, after so brief a contact, proved not only a vitally important factor for himself but also an additional common bond with Winston Churchill.

Mindful of this fact I spent some time in the Roosevelt Memorial Library at Hyde Park, New York, and also visited at length the mansion itself where that dramatic meeting of the week-end of 10 – 11 June 1939 had taken place. Here I was much beholden to the kindness of Mrs Roosevelt, who took me through the house, showed me the various rooms allotted to the King and Queen and to Mr Mackenzie King, and also the site of the near catastrophe in the library where, after dinner, a black butler imported from the White House had missed his footing and had arrived at the Queen's feet in a sitting posture and an ever-spreading lake of ice-cubes and the contents of broken decanters, siphons and bottles of mineral water. It was under her auspices, too, that I was shown the cottage around which had occurred the famous picnic where, to the shocked horror of some, the British sovereigns were served with hot dogs.

There was one transient bad moment which I experienced, however, during this remarkable visit. Mrs Roosevelt gave a buffet-luncheon for me at her own Hyde Park cottage, to which she had invited her youngest son and his wife and others who had been present in some capacity or other during the Royal visit. Mrs Roosevelt felt constrained to make an introductory speech explaining who I was and why I was there, which would have been of the greatest value had she not begun her remarks with the words, 'I would like to introduce Mr Wheeler-Bennett who has come all the way from England to see us because he is writing the official life of – Mr Winston Churchill'! I had to wait until she had finished her homily, which continued for some time, before seizing the opportunity to explain the real motive for my presence.

Though King George's relations with President Truman never achieved the intimacy of those with his predecessor, they did have a memorable meeting in U.S.S. *Augusta* in Plymouth Bay on 2 August 1945, and a year or two later the President was host to Princess Elizabeth and Prince Philip during their first visit to the North American continent. I was therefore anxious to see him, and the circumstances of our meeting were unusual.

Mr Truman, after the termination of his presidency, received an honorary degree from the University of Oxford and it was at the Vice-Chancellor's garden-party – I think at New College – that, thanks to the kindness of Sir Oliver Franks, who had recently retired as British Ambassador in Washington, I was presented to him. Mr Truman was his own splendidly direct self. In the briefest possible way I explained why I would like a talk with him. 'Come to breakfast,' he said hospitably, adding, somewhat to my dismay, 'to-morrow at 8.30 at the Savoy.'

I then made my manners to Mrs Truman, saying, banally

enough, that I hoped she had not found too wearisome the various ceremonies which render the day of encaenia at Oxford quite one of the most exhausting imaginable. To my huge delight she replied with the immortal words, which I had often read and heard on the movies but had never before encountered, as it were, in the flesh: 'My feet are killing me.' How well I knew how she felt. Having found her a chair, I pressed a glass of iced tea into her hand and fled for home, there to pack and catch the evening train to London.

Bright and early next morning I called the Truman suite from the lobby of the Savoy, expecting, I confess, to be summoned upstairs. On the contrary, I was instructed to wait in the lobby and very shortly thereafter, for Mr Truman was a punctual man, the President emerged from the lift escorted by Stanley Woodward, formerly *chef de protocole* at the State Department and American Ambassador to Canada, and at that time bear-leading Mr and Mrs Truman through their European tour.

Stanley was an old friend from Charlottesville days and his presence gave me encouragement, but what I was not prepared for was a general move to the Grill Room. There are gayer and more amusing places in which to eat breakfast than the Savoy Grill but the experience must surely be unique. It was rather like breakfasting with Eurydice among the shades of Hades. The revellers of supper time had vanished leaving what seemed to be acres of tables shrouded in cloths which had been turned up over them preparatory to their being laid for luncheon.

Quite undeterred, however, Mr Truman sat down between Stanley Woodward and myself, conversed spicily on general subjects and consumed a healthy meal, while at the other end of the table, separated from us by several places, were two or three figures like supernumerary characters in a Chekhov play, who remained silent, ate hugely, and exhibited all the detectable features of being 'gum-shoe men'

(U.S. government detectives) charged with Mr Truman's protection.

At the close of this strange repast we went up to the suite, and Mr Truman was affability itself, answering my questions fully and with gusto and throwing in such spirited comments as, 'I certainly was glad to hear your King take the mickey out of Bill Leahy over the atom bomb.' This indeed had been true, for the Admiral, who had been the President's Chief of Staff, had expressed the greatest scepticism whether the bomb would work, and King George, who was among the best informed men on this whole matter, had offered him a bet on its success.

After this unusual meeting I saw Mr Truman again in Washington on several occasions, on one of which I told him that I had asked Lord Attlee whether he had ever had any qualms of conscience about dropping the first bomb on Hiroshima and had received an emphatic negative. Had Mr Truman, I now asked, ever lost any sleep, either at the time or subsequently, at having given the order? 'Not a wink,' replied the President. 'It was my plain duty and I did it. But I'll tell you what did worry me at that time, and that was that, if anything happened to me, Ed Stettinius would be President of the United States.'*

I am confident that President Truman will be numbered among the greatest leaders of the United States. He was essentially a man of his own making. He differed from his predecessor in background, character and approach. President Roosevelt's ancestry was that of the aristocratic patroon families: President Truman came of virile, pioneer stock. President Roosevelt had reached the White House through the Governor's chair in Albany, New York: President Truman had begun his political career in the Pendergast machine in

---

*It should be remembered that at this time the Secretary of State — then Mr Stettinius — was next in succession to the Presidency after the Vice-President. The Twenty-fifth Amendment to the Constitution has changed this to the Speaker of the House of Representatives.

Kansas City, Missouri. Without the subtlety and agility of mind and the blinding charm of Roosevelt, Truman matched him in courage, in vision and in bull-dog determination and, when necessary, excelled him in ruthlessness. Their principles and precepts were identical, but whereas Roosevelt arrived at his uncanny understanding of American public opinion by means of an almost feminine intuition, Truman derived his own keen perception from within himself, through an upwelling of his own inner consciousness. Truly the comment of a New York weekly magazine, that 'President Roosevelt was *for* the people: President Truman *is* the people', was not far off the mark.

The thirty-second President of the United States personified that combination of fundamental toughness, commonsense and goodness of heart which comprises the average American. He was more forthright, less devious, than President Roosevelt, and by his very forthrightness he prevented the American people from slipping back into the myopic self-righteousness which had afflicted them after the First World War.

As between Mr Truman and his predecessor I know whom I would have chosen as a partner for a tiger-shoot.

When at length I sat down at Garsington to the actual writing of my task I had a very clear impression of the man in whose life and times I had been immersed for the last four years. He was a man for whom fate had originally designed a very different destiny from that which he ultimately fulfilled with such conspicuous success. He was every inch a second son; one who would have been supremely happy in the love and devotion of his home life with his wife and children, yet ready to serve his country by such imaginative means as his Boys' Camps which he himself initiated. He was unschooled in statecraft. He did not desire to be involved in the great problems which concern a head of state. He was content to leave these matters to his elder brother. He was essentially a dutiful and useful citizen. He shunned the limelight.

All this became apparent to me in my study of his early life. But there was something else. His disinclination for public life became the greater because of the severe stammer from which he had suffered from childhood. How well I understood this physical disability and its inevitable psychological reaction. As I have described in *Knaves, Fools and Heroes*, I too had experienced the discouragement caused by the failures of successive specialists to effect a cure, and I, too, had suffered the despair of the chronic stammerer, and the secret dread that the hidden root of the malady lay in the mind rather than in the body.

Stranger still was the discovery that I also, at almost the same time as the Duke of York, had had rekindled within me the embers of hope at the hands of the same voice-therapist, Lionel Logue, an Australian who, having begun his education and training as an engineer, had found within himself the gift of healing.

Logue's approach was both physical and psychological. His presence and personality inspired confidence, but by the very simplicity and sincerity of his nature rather than by any cultivated 'bedside manner'. Those who sought his professional advice felt immediately that not only did he believe in his own power of healing but he was able to inspire them with a similar belief both in him and in themselves. With a complete understanding of his own subject, he knew that the stammerer's first fear was of seeming 'different' from others. His first objective, therefore, was to convince his patient that stammerers could be entirely normal persons with a perfectly curable complaint.

'There comes to every stammerer,' I remember his once saying to me, 'a moment of choice. Either he can surrender to his stammer, shun society, and retire into an ivory tower from which he may produce great studies which will increase the general knowledge of mankind and perhaps even benefit its lot. He may be a good and useful person but he will never be cured of his stammer. The other course is to make society suffer! Stammer at them if you have something to say until you can compel them to listen to you. Scorn their mocking: only fools will mock you. Discourage even the well-intentioned from helping you. Stand on your own feet. You will gain confidence and you will eventually lose your stammer.'

His physical treatment consisted of teaching the stammerer to breathe correctly, if necessary developing his lungs by physical exercises to control his diaphragmatic rhythm. The fundamental secret of success was that, whereas from the first contact he caused the patient to believe in the certainty of a cure, he made it absolutely clear that this certainty depended as much upon the patient as upon himself, and even more. 'There is only one person who can cure you and that is yourself,' was a favourite dictum. 'I can tell you what to do but only you can do it.' The patient, having acquired initial confidence, was thereby brought into active partnership in his own treatment and was made to see that the ultimate good of a successful cure was his for the gaining.

This curious affinity of suffering in combating a common disability made it appreciably easier for me to understand the distress which the Duke suffered in the last months of his brother's reign at the close of 1936. Indeed, no one who reads his own poignant contemporary account of the abdication crisis, which I found among his papers and which is printed in *King George VI*, can fail to understand with the deepest compassion the agony of apprehension with which he watched the unrelenting approach of that moment when he would have to take up the burdens and onus of kingship which his brother was preparing to lay down.

Only a staunch fidelity to duty and the devotion of the Duchess of York brought him through the searing time of testing. Yet once the responsibility was his, he grasped it unshrinkingly with both hands, gallantly accepting the destiny which, in the event, was to prove him one of England's best and wisest kings.

Years later, in a flurry of sentimentality which attended the death of the Duke of Windsor in 1972, the then Archbishop of York, Dr Donald Coggan (now Primate of All England) summed up in a letter to *The Times* on 7 June, with the beauty of simple language and the perspective of history, the circumstances of King George VI's succession:

The death and burial of the Duke of Windsor are now past, and will soon fall into their place in the long history of the British people. But before their memory is dimmed one observer would be grateful for the courtesy of your columns to express surprise at an omission in the press which must have distressed many readers in recent weeks.

Practically nothing has been said of the self discipline and stern sense of duty which led one man to shoulder a task which was as unwelcome as it was unsought. Very little mention has been made of the lady without whom that burden would have proved intolerable, but through whose encouragement he was enabled to fulfil his duty to the end. That man and that gracious lady held the nation firm when the abdication had shaken it to its foundations.

We should all do well to ponder again the relevant chapters in *King George VI, His Life and Reign* which Sir John Wheeler-Bennett has written with such penetrating insight and historical accuracy.

Yours faithfully,

DONALD EBOR

As I wrote about the King I became a sincere admirer. I had never known him personally and, before I assumed my task as his biographer, I confess he had seemed to me to be something of a colourless if worthy figure. I soon had to alter this idea. Far from insipid, King George was a vivid personality, with a wealth of pragmatic commonsense, foresight and good judgement which caused him to prove an asset of great value to his ministers and advisers. In addition to his immense degree of duty to his kingly functions in peace and war, he had an awareness of humanity which took him to the hearts of his people at home and of his troops abroad. Moreover, his sense of humour was, judged from every source of evidence, highly developed and capable of becoming rollicking. Sense and sensibility may be said to epitomise his character. But the prevailing source of strength, in trial or calm, in happiness or adversity, was the abiding, never-failing love of his Queen.

My task was finally completed. *King George VI, His Life and Reign* was published by Macmillan on 13 October 1958 – my fifty-sixth birthday. Six years of my life had been consumed in the most fascinating task which I have ever undertaken, and I can never be sufficiently grateful to the Queen and to Queen Elizabeth the Queen Mother for entrusting me with so responsible an assignment. But I could never have accomplished my enterprise without the unstinted help of Tommy Lascelles and later of his successors Michael Adeane and Martin Charteris, who smoothed my way, encouraged my efforts and gave generously of their knowledge; of Owen Morshead, whose delightfully intellectual humour and wide knowledge made him a kindly arbiter, as was his deputy and subsequent successor, Robin Mackworth-Young. Norman Brook, then Secretary to the Cabinet, guided my navigation among the rocks and shoals of the Official Secrets Act and of Whitehall in general. No writer could have been blessed with more loyal friends and counsellors, and no writer needed them more. For, however fascinating it may be, royal biography, like matrimony, 'is not to be entered into inadvisedly or lightly; but reverently, discreetly, advisedly, soberly and in the fear of God'.

I fully expected that, when I had tidied up my affairs at

Buckingham Palace and had received the thanks of the Queen, my connection with the Court would end. I had become a regular at the palace over the past six years and had made many friends there, including the police, the detectives and footmen, all of whom were most kind to me. All this now was over. It was an odd feeling of starting one's life again.

It may be imagined, therefore, with what surprise and gratification I received word from Sir Michael Adeane – on 11 February 1959, just a week after I had left Buckingham Palace for good – that the Queen had decided to create a new position in her Household, namely that of Historical Adviser to the Royal Archives, and to appoint me as its first incumbent. It is an office which I have held ever since, and Her Majesty, who had knighted me and appointed me to the Royal Victorian Order on 4 February 1959, promoted me to Knight Grand Cross in the same Order – her own – on 16 March 1974.

On my seventieth birthday my nephews and nieces most sweetly marked the occasion by presenting me with my portrait by Juliet Pannett, which formed the frontispiece for *Knaves, Fools and Heroes*. Ruth and I celebrated with a cocktail-party of friends and relations in the Great Subscription Room of Brooks's, at which Harold Macmillan proposed my health and Alec Douglas-Home started them singing 'Happy Birthday'. I am told that our revelry was heard in St James's Street and that people smiled. It was a happy day.

Epilogue

To review one's life as I have done in these three successive volumes of recollections, though interesting for the writer, is yet not an entirely joyful experience. Standards of comparison inevitably obtrude themselves and one is always in danger of thinking that nothing today is as pleasant as it was when one was young. (Perhaps, indeed, one is not wholly wrong in this!)

I spent my childhood in the age of security; I was filled with adolescent enthusiastic idealism at the time of the First World War, and I attained my manhood at a time when we still believed in the possibility of building a world safe for democracy, having fought and won a war to end war.

The sequel has been a traumatic one. Our early dreams have proved to be but a chimera, a euphoric fantasy. Twice in the last fifty years we have seen our hopes for the success of an international peace-keeping organisation wither under the icy blasts of reality in Geneva and in New York, until today we have reached the nadir of irony in that our main guarantee of world peace lies in our knowledge that even the victor is vanquished in a nuclear war. 'Yet,' as my old friend, that great Canadian statesman, the late Lester Pearson has warned us, 'peace rests uneasily on a hydrogen bomb; and an intercontinental missile is a weak foundation for lasting security.' Despite this guarantee there is a menacing sense of *déjà vu*.

It is written of the Duke of Wellington that, in the course of one of the brief lulls during the battle of Waterloo, he perceived some act of gallantry in the French lines where the wounded were being evacuated, and raised his low-crowned cocked hat in recognition. 'Whom are you saluting, Duke?' asked one of his entourage. 'I salute the courage and devotion of an age that is no longer ours,' was the reply.

This for me is the expression of my own reflections. We live, alas, in an age in which violence is rife, in which politics are destructive rather than constructive, and in which standards of conduct, in comparison with the higher codes of my youth – both public and private, at home and in the world at large – have not only changed, but have changed perceptibly for the worse. There are no giants left in our world, and I was born and lived much of my life in an age of giants. I see a great procession before me, some of whom I have been privileged to know – Arthur Balfour, Herbert Asquith, David Lloyd George, Stanley Baldwin, Anthony Eden, Winston Churchill, Clement Attlee and Harold Macmillan. All these had one salient characteristic in common. They were leaders; they could command a following; they shared the element of greatness.

Amid this gloom, however, there are compensations and one clings to them. Among the things that one appreciates more and more as age increases is the gift of friendship. In the course of a fairly long life I have made a host of acquaintances and have been blessed with a considerable number of friends in all walks of life. I thank God for all of them, both those whose company I can still enjoy and those who are but happy memories.

But over and above all else am I deeply grateful for the love and compassion, the fun and the understanding, the tolerance and the comfort which my beloved Ruth has given me over more than thirty years.

Index

172

INDEX

INDEX